Key Stage 1

ICT

Alan Rodgers and Angella Streluk

CONTENTS

Introduction   3
Curriculum Planners   6

Communicating information   8

UNIT **1** Introduction to using the keyboard   10

UNIT **2** Introduction to word processing   12

UNIT **3** Word processing skills   14

UNIT **4** Early painting activities   16

UNIT **5** Developing painting skills   18

UNIT **6** Musical composition   20

UNIT **7** E-mail introduction   22

Handling Data   24

UNIT **8** Sorting activities   26

UNIT **9** Introduction to classification   28

UNIT **10** Creating and using pictograms   30

UNIT **11** Sorting diagrams   32

UNIT **12** Binary databases   34

UNIT **13** Searching and sorting   36

UNIT **14** Graphing data   38

Modelling and control   40

UNIT **15** Using a floor robot   42

UNIT **16** Giving instructions   44

UNIT **17** Programming a floor robot   46

UNIT **18** Introduction to *Logo*   48

UNIT **19** Drawing shapes   50

UNIT **20** An introduction to modelling   52

UNIT **21** Adventures and simulations   54

UNIT **22** Everyday technology   56

CD-ROM and Internet   58

UNIT **23** Recognising information   60

UNIT **24** Using a CD-ROM   62

UNIT **25** Features of CD-ROMs   64

UNIT **26** An introduction to the Internet   66

UNIT **27** Using the Internet   68

UNIT **28** Simple multimedia   70

Copymasters 1–56   72

Using *Learning Targets* with the Scottish
5–14 National Guidelines for ICT

(inside back cover)

INTRODUCTION

This book aims to support the teaching of ICT by providing clear lessons which focus on specific objectives. The activities are grouped into broad areas of ICT, but it is also hoped that skills can be transferred from one activity to another. The introduction to each section offers further guidance on choice and use of resources and more specific issues. Support in using ICT in the broader curriculum also brings a more meaningful approach to the subject. At the same time ICT is a subject to be given time in its own right in order to develop the skills necessary to apply it.

When teaching ICT to young children opposing considerations must be taken into account. One is that some of the concepts covered in the ICT curriculum are very complex; think of the perceived complexities when just beginning ICT. Another consideration seems directly opposed to this. Young children have grown up in a world full of technology. Some things which seem complex to us are second nature to them. If care is taken with the ICT curriculum, then these opposing points can co-exist to yield excellent results.

How ICT is taught depends both on the resources available and on the philosophy of the school. If there is access to a computer suite ICT can almost always be taught in a whole-class lesson. If this opportunity is not available, the initial input is likely to be a whole-class activity, followed by group work timetabled so far as is practicable. The latter can have the disadvantage of removing the children's experience to a much later time than the initial input. This also removes the advantage of shared experience, with children learning from each other as they work on an activity. The ideal situation would be to have access to both computer suites and classroom-based computers. Other lessons, using floor robots or concept keyboards, would, by necessity, be small group activities, unless the school has enough floor robots to make a whole-class activity practical.

Although it is hoped that adequate hardware resources are available, not all resources need to be hi-tech or expensive. The use of punch cards to introduce databases is a good example. There are many other activities which we have suggested that help to develop ICT but do not require a computer.

Software which enables you to control certain aspects, such as the ability to print, is increasingly available as software companies become more aware of educational needs. This means that the practical aspects of ICT, such as the economic use of paper and printer ink, become more manageable. You can make available or prohibit certain functions such as printing and saving. This is done through an interface specially prepared for the teacher, and protected by a password. It is also worth remembering that having more software available does not necessarily mean that it will be used to good effect. There are instances where standard software, not specifically written with educational establishments in mind, can be adapted. Using *PowerPoint* for creating a binary database is an example of this.

There are still many concerns which stem from other curriculum areas. When teachers take such care in introducing certain forms of letters to young children can we reasonably expect them to cope with an upper case keyboard? Should young pupils have a keyboard with lower case letters? If it is a class-based computer that is being used, the keyboard can be replaced, or special stickers can be used. In a shared computer suite, especially shared by key stages, they may just have to manage.

It is important that the teacher also uses the skills being taught. You should set the example of using either *shift* key and not the *caps lock* key when typing capital letters. It is important not only to put spaces after words, but to also put spaces after punctuation. You need to be aware that using the *return/enter* key to start a new paragraph is a big step, as at first children may be tempted to use the spacebar to move the cursor onto a new line.

How this book is organised

The sections

This book is divided into 4 sections:
- Communicating information
- Handling information
- Modelling and control
- CD-ROM and Internet

Each one provides units which cover aspects of the Programme of study. Each section begins with a short overview covering the focus of the units, resource implications and teaching issues. There is also a page of cross-curricular links for each section which offers other ideas to develop within the areas of ICT covered in the section.

The units

Sections are sub-divided into units. Each unit covers a number of requirements from the National Curriculum Programme of study. The Learning Targets state explicitly what the children should aim to know or be able to do by the end of the unit and provide you with clear, assessable objectives to teach.

There is no determined order in which to teach the units although they have been written to show continuity and progression within the main areas of ICT. There are usually two or three units building up the skills and knowledge for each type of software. In general units at the beginning of a sub-section are easier and difficulty builds up incrementally. An indication of the age-appropriateness of a unit is given at the start of that unit.

The sessions

Units are composed of 2 or 3 teaching sessions which, in general, increase in complexity. There is an introduction where the aim of the lesson is put in context. This is generally followed by a hands-on teacher demonstration at the computer. An icon shows where this takes place. In most cases this leads on to the children trying the activity at the computer although occasionally they need to work at their tables before moving to the computer. Once the practical tasks have been completed, the class comes together again to bring the lesson to a close.

The timing of the sessions will vary according to the resources available in the school. Where there is a network of computers available, a session will generally be the equivalent of an ICT lesson. In schools where children are working with a classroom computer, the sessions at the computer will of course be much longer in order to give every child/group of children adequate time to complete the practical task.

The copymasters

Photocopiable sheets accompany every unit. They provide activities, or a means of recording information; many could also be used by the teacher for assessment of understanding. References are made to the copymasters in the lesson plans.

Explicit targets for achievement in every session

The concise subject knowledge you need

Crystal clear lesson plan layouts

The full range of teaching strategies

Rigorous and practical activities

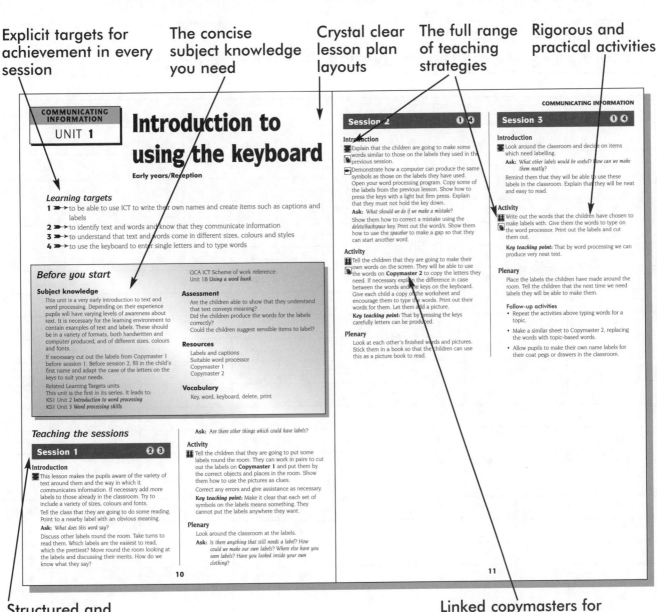

Structured and carefully paced sessions

Linked copymasters for differentiated practice and assessment

The symbol key

(3)	Indicates the number of the Learning Target covered in each session or lesson
	Computer activity
	Teacher demonstration
	Interactive whole class teaching session
	Group work session
	Individual within a group work session
	Pair work session
	Individual session

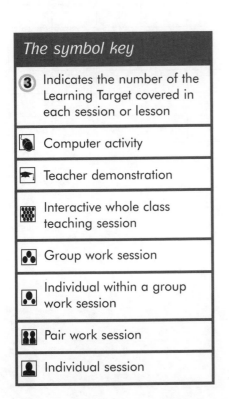

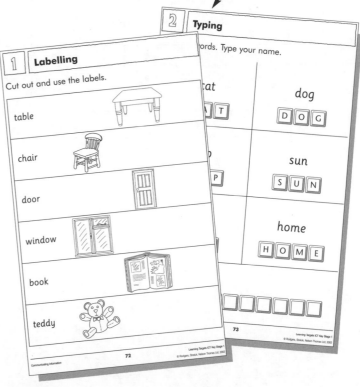

Unit No.	1			2				3		4		
	a	b	c	a	b	c	d	a	b	a	b	c
1		•		•								
2		•		•						•		
3		•	•	•						•		
4		•		•							•	
5		•	•	•			•		•			
6		•					•	•			•	
7				•				•				
8			•									
9		•									•	
10	•	•	•		•					•		
11		•		•				•			•	
12			•				•					
13			•		•		•					
14		•	•						•			
15						•	•					
16						•	•				•	•
17					•	•	•			•	•	•
18						•	•			•	•	•
19			•			•	•			•	•	•
20							•				•	
21							•			•	•	•
22						•				•		
23	•	•	•									
24	•		•									
25	•		•		•			•				
26			•									
27			•									
28		•			•			•	•	•		

Curriculum planner
QCA/DfES Scheme of work: ICT

Unit No.	1A Introduction to modelling	1B Using a word bank	1C The information around us	1D Labelling and classifying	1E Representing information graphically: pictograms	1F Understanding instructions and making things happen	2A Writing stories: communicating information using text	2B Creating pictures	2C Finding information	2D Routes: controlling a floor turtle	2E Questions and answers
1		●									
2		●									
3							●				
4								●			
5								●			
6						●					
7											
8				●							
9				●							
10					●						
11			●	●	●						
12											
13											
14											●
15						●					
16						●					
17										●	
18											
19											
20	●										
21	●										
22						●					
23			●								
24									●		
25									●		
26			●								
27									●		
28											

COMMUNICATING INFORMATION

Units 1–7

These units deal largely with the creative elements of ICT. They include word processing, painting and musical composition. Also included is an introduction to e-mail, which makes use of word processing skills.

Resource Issues

There are concerns about Key Stage 1 pupils using standard ICT equipment. Those concerns regarding the use of upper and lower case letters are covered in the Introduction (p.4). There is also concern over the use of standard fonts. A lot of trouble is taken by teachers to consistently use letters easily recognisable to young children. Should a special font be used for children of this age when using a computer? If this is felt to be important, one of the best fonts to use is *Sassoon* font. This is specially designed for primary school children, and can be bought with several variations to choose from.

The word processor to be used at this level needs to be chosen with care. Some programs, such as MS*Word*, require the user to press *enter* to move down the page. Child–friendly programs, such as *Textease* 2000, allow the user to click anywhere and type immediately. Providing a word bank to aid children is also important. This can be done in many software packages including *Clicker*4 and *Textease* 2000. These can also incorporate pictures which help children to identify the words.

There are several ways of acquiring outline images for use with children. They can be scanned from a printed image. *Clip art* often comes in outline for activities like the one in Unit 4. Otherwise, drawing a purpose-made image, using the *shape* and *line* tools, can be quite easy. Check that the *flood fill* tool will work with these images.

Teaching Issues

The rate at which the children progress in ICT during Key Stage 1 is rapid. However, when they start their ICT work they may need to be taught very fundamental skills. For this reason it is important that the software can be used at a variety of levels of difficulty. There is more about this in the Introduction (p.3).

At this young age developing correct word processing habits is very important. You need to set an example by using good habits then, hopefully, the children will use them as well. These important skills are also included in the Introduction.

When using e-mail with children it is important to make sure that the correspondents are trusted people. Children should never give their surnames or pictures to people via e-mail unless they have permission from parents or guardians. Bearing this in mind it is still an excellent tool to use as part of the curriculum.

There are two different types of musical composition programs. Unit 6 makes use of a program which is based on the accepted musical representation of notes on staves. One such program is RM *Music Explorer*. This progresses through levels, starting with basic icons representing notes and moving on to complete musical notation. The other type of program is equally useful. With *Compose World Junior* the children arrange phrases of music which are represented as pictures. This enables them to experiment to find a combination of phrases and repeats which are pleasing to the ear.

Ideas for Cross-curricular Teaching

English

Using word processing gives an excellent means of planning and drafting. Writing frames are easy to construct and to use in language work.

- Sequence stories
- Write descriptions

Maths

Although areas other than Communicating Information will be more relevant, there are some links with this section.

- Draw, paint and label 2D shapes (also use *Clip art*)
- Use a word bank to link shapes to the shape names

Science

Writing reports and sequencing events greatly benefit from the provision of vocabulary and images provided through ICT.

- Sequence the life cycle of a plant
- Write a description of how to care for a pet
- Paint pictures of things we can smell

Design and Technology

Word processing skills can be used in a variety of ways. Paint packages can also be useful for you when presenting images of the children's models.

- Produce a set of labels for a display of models
- Make a list of the materials needed for a project
- Load images of models into a paint package or desktop publishing program and ask the children to label them

History

All the skills covered in the Communicating Information units are helpful in History work.

- Produce a museum leaflet
- Create musical compositions on a historical theme

Geography

Making observations of places, environments, and features could involve text, images or both.

- Create a guide book for a location
- Use a paint package to depict various buildings
- Make a map and label it using a paint package

Art

Although using ICT in Art is not statutory at KS1 it gives children a chance to be creative in a different medium.

- Produce pictures in the style of an artist being studied
- Add colour to an image already drawn in outline
- Use a word bank to describe what the children think about the work of an artist being studied

Music

Although using the musical composition program is the most relevant activity, pupils might also be asked to record their feelings about a piece of music.

- Create music to go with a topic
- Explore the effects of fast and slow music
- Write a description of the mood of a piece of music

Introduction to using the keyboard

Early years/Reception

Learning targets

1 ➤➤ to be able to use ICT to write their own names and create items such as captions and labels

2 ➤➤ to identify text and words and know that they communicate information

3 ➤➤ to understand that text and words come in different sizes, colours and styles

4 ➤➤ to use the keyboard to enter single letters and to type words

Before you start

Subject knowledge

This unit is a very early introduction to text and word processing. Depending on their experience pupils will have varying levels of awareness about text. It is necessary for the learning environment to contain examples of text and labels. These should be in a variety of formats, both handwritten and computer produced, and of different sizes, colours and fonts.

If necessary cut out the labels from Copymaster 1 before session 1. Before session 2, fill in the child's first name and adapt the case of the letters on the keys to suit your needs.

Related Learning Targets units:
This unit is the first in its series. It leads to:
KS1 Unit 2 *Introduction to word processing*
KS1 Unit 3 *Word processing skills*

QCA ICT Scheme of work reference:
Unit 1B *Using a word bank*

Assessment

Are the children able to show that they understand that text conveys meaning?
Did the children produce the words for the labels correctly?
Could the children suggest sensible items to label?

Resources

Labels and captions
Suitable word processor
Copymaster 1
Copymaster 2

Vocabulary

Key, word, keyboard, delete, print

Teaching the sessions

Session 1 ② ③

Introduction

▦ This lesson makes the pupils aware of the variety of text around them and the way in which it communicates information. If necessary add more labels to those already in the classroom. Try to include a variety of sizes, colours and fonts.

Tell the class that they are going to do some reading. Point to a nearby label with an obvious meaning.

Ask: *What does this word say?*

Discuss other labels round the room. Take turns to read them. Which labels are the easiest to read, which the prettiest? Move round the room looking at the labels and discussing their merits. How do we know what they say?

Ask: *Are there other things which could have labels?*

Activity

👥 Tell the children that they are going to put some labels round the room. They can work in pairs to cut out the labels on **Copymaster 1** and put them by the correct objects and places in the room. Show them how to use the pictures as clues.

Correct any errors and give assistance as necessary.

Key teaching point: Make it clear that each set of symbols on the labels means something. They cannot put the labels anywhere they want.

Plenary

Look around the classroom at the labels.

Ask: *Is there anything that still needs a label? How could we make our own labels? Where else have you seen labels? Have you looked inside your own clothing?*

Session 2

Introduction

Explain that the children are going to make some words similar to those on the labels they used in the previous session.

Demonstrate how a computer can produce the same symbols as those on the labels they have used. Open your word processing program. Copy some of the labels from the previous lesson. Show how to press the keys with a light but firm press. Explain that they must not hold the key down.

Ask: *What should we do if we make a mistake?*

Show them how to correct a mistake using the *delete/backspace* key. Print out the word/s. Show them how to use the *spacebar* to make a gap so that they can start another word.

Activity

Tell the children that they are going to make their own words on the screen. They will be able to use the words on **Copymaster 2** to copy the letters they need. If necessary explain the difference in case between the words and the keys on the keyboard. Give each child a copy of the worksheet and encourage them to type the words. Print out their words for them. Let them add a picture.

Key teaching point: That by pressing the keys carefully letters can be produced.

Plenary

Look at each other's finished words and pictures. Stick them in a book so that the children can use this as a picture book to read.

Session 3

Introduction

Look around the classroom and decide on items which need labelling.

> **Ask:** *What other labels would be useful? How can we make them neatly?*

Remind them that they will be able to use these labels in the classroom. Explain that they will be neat and easy to read.

Activity

Write out the words that the children have chosen to make labels with. Give them the words to type on the word processor. Print out the labels and cut them out.

Key teaching point: That by word processing we can produce very neat text.

Plenary

Place the labels the children have made around the room. Tell the children that the next time we need labels they will be able to make them.

Follow-up activities

• Repeat the activities above typing words for a topic.

• Make a similar sheet to Copymaster 2, replacing the words with topic-based words.

• Allow pupils to make their own name labels for their coat pegs or drawers in the classroom.

Introduction to word processing

Year 1

Learning targets

1 ➥ to be able to use text to develop their ideas
2 ➥ to use a word bank to create simple sentences
3 ➥ to produce text on the screen that is clear and error-free

Before you start

Subject knowledge

You will need to prepare a word bank using the software available. Prepare one set using words that link to a current topic. Exclude words that the children can confidently spell, such as 'a' or 'the'. Also prepare a word bank to go with Copymaster 4. These words can include both nouns and verbs.

The children have entered text using the keyboard in Unit 1. They will now combine this with using words in a word bank. This means that the children can simply click on the word and it will be entered in their text for them. Pictures can also be used for words which are easy to illustrate. A lot of software comes with files which can be used for the more common topics covered in Key Stage 1.

Related Learning Targets units:
KS1 Unit 1 *Introduction to using the keyboard*
KS1 Unit 3 *Word processing skills*
QCA ICT Scheme of work reference:
Unit 1B *Using a word bank*

Assessment

Were the children able to combine words from the word bank with text typed using the keyboard? Can the children correct errors?
Are the children confident that they can produce neat text using a computer?

Resources

Word bank program
Ready prepared word banks to fit a current topic and one for Copymaster 4
Copymaster 3
Copymaster 4

Vocabulary

Word bank, key, text, spacebar, delete/backspace, print, printer

Teaching the sessions

Session 1 ①

Introduction

▦ Look at a piece of printed text and a piece of handwritten text. Identify the key differences. In the printed one the letters are all the same, the size matches and the writing is clear and dark. The handwritten text may be more interesting and can have extra flourishes added.

Ask: *If we wanted to produce something for everybody to read which one would be better?*

Activity

👥 Show the children **Copymaster 3**. Explain to the children that they are going to produce a piece of text to go with the picture on this worksheet. Discuss the picture. They are going to be provided with the words they need. They will need to put the words into the right order to make text to fit the picture.

Ask: *What could you write using these words? Why might we want the words printed for us?*

Ask the children to cut out the words and stick them under the picture to make some writing. Ask them to try to make the writing fit the picture.

Key teaching point: Emphasise the importance of thinking about which word needs to be chosen next.

Plenary

Share the writing done by the children.

Ask: *How many people stuck the same words in the same order? Can you all understand each other's text?*

Session 2 ① ②

Introduction

Explain that once again they are going to use words to create their own piece of writing. This time they will not need scissors and glue. Set up the word bank on the computer. Show them how the words are already on the computer screen for them.

Ask: *How do you think we will make the words appear on the screen?*

Demonstrate how clicking on the words at the bottom of the screen puts the text onto the screen. Show how words can also be typed in using the keyboard. Revise how to correct errors using the *delete/backspace* key. Show how to use the *spacebar* to make a space between words. Read through the topic words in the word bank. Ask for suggestions of sentences that could be made using these words.

Activity

Ask the children to use the word bank to produce some writing about the topic they are currently doing. Ask them to correct any errors they make, and to remember to press the keys on the keyboard firmly but without holding them down.

Print out the text and ask them to add a picture to go with the text.

Key teaching point: That words from the word bank can be combined with text typed using the keyboard.

Plenary

Ask the children to read each other's text. Is it easier to read now that it has been printed out?

Ask: *Could this work be used to make a display for the topic?*

Session 3 ① ② ③

Introduction

Show the children **Copymaster 4**. Remind the children of how they used a word bank to make a piece of writing. Discuss the picture.

Ask: *What words might you need to write about this picture?*

Briefly demonstrate how to enter text using the word bank and keyboard.

Activity

Use the word bank to produce a piece of text to go with the picture on Copymaster 4. Check the work to see that there are no errors. Print out the text and affix it to the picture.

Key teaching point: That words entered in this way are more easily readable.

Plenary

Ask the children what other activities a word bank could be used for.

Follow-up activities

• Use the above activity regularly to support other curriculum areas.

• Write a series of captions to tell a story the children know well.

• Send 'letters' to each other using a classroom post box.

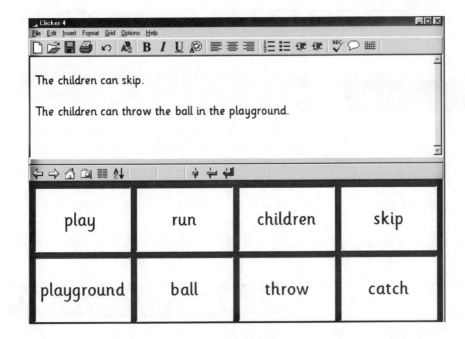

A *Clicker* 4 word bank being used for an activity which could go with Copymaster 3. These are very simple to set up.

Word processing skills

Year 2

Learning targets

1 ➤➤ to be able to present their completed work effectively

2 ➤➤ to identify where the *return/enter* key should be used in text, and why

3 ➤➤ to use appropriate techniques to ensure that their writing is clear, well presented and error-free

Before you start

Subject knowledge

The children should be increasingly familiar with the layout of the keyboard. They should already have experienced using a word processor, both with a word bank and by using the keys on the keyboard. It is important in this unit that you should not only look at the finished product, but also see how it is achieved. This means that bad habits are not reinforced, but corrected before it is too late.

Related Learning Targets units:
KS1 Unit 2 *Introduction to word processing*
KS2 Unit 1 *Recipe instructions*
QCA ICT Scheme of work reference:
Unit 2A *Writing stories: communicating information using text*

Assessment

Is the final piece of work presented satisfactorily?
Are pupils confident in when and why to use the *return/enter* key?
Are the children able to correct errors?

Resources

Word processor
The poem from Copymaster 5 presented as a word processor file, with no capital letters or returns
Copymaster 5
Copymaster 6

Vocabulary

Shift, spacebar, return/enter, delete, backspace, Caps Lock

Teaching the sessions

Session 1 ① ③

Introduction

Ask: *Why do we use a computer to produce text?*

 Encourage answers referring to the ability to correct, neatness of the finished text, the fact that we can change it later and print multiple copies. Open a word processing program.

Revise how to enter text, use *delete/backspace*, use *enter* and use the *spacebar*.

Show the children how to use *shift* to make a capital letter. Discourage the use of *Caps Lock* unless making a poster completely in upper case letters.

Ask: *When do we use a capital letter in our writing?*

Revise the use of upper case letters for the first letter of sentences and names.

Activity

Ask the children to work in pairs to type a sentence about their partner. Check each other's work. When both have typed a sentence, print out the text.

Key teaching point: That *shift*, not *Caps Lock* is the way to type single capital letters.

Plenary

Ask the children to read out their sentences. Ask the children who their sentences are about.

Ask: *Does the sentence have a capital letter at the beginning? Does your name have a capital letter at the beginning?*

Session 2 ① ②

Introduction

Show the children a short four lined poem, typed in using a word processor.

Ask: *How did these words get onto a new line?*

Demonstrate how to use the *return/enter* key to move the cursor onto a new line. Show how to move the text back up by using *delete/backspace*.

Activity

Look at the poem on **Copymaster 5**. Read the poem with the children.

Ask: *What makes this writing look like a poem?*

Pick out the rhyming words. The children may circle them or highlight them. Look at the way they appear at the ends of the lines. Look at the capital letters at the beginnings of the lines.

Ask: *Have you seen other poems which look like this?*

Load the prepared text of the poem with no capital letters or returns. Ask the children to modify the text by putting the cursor in the right places and pressing *return/enter*. Ask them to change some of the letters to capital letters to make it like the poem on Copymaster 5.

Print out the text and illustrate the poem.

Key teaching point: That it is easy to use *return/enter* to move to a new line in the text.

Plenary

Compare the printouts with Copymaster 5. Look especially at the capital letters and new lines.

Ask: *Are the returns and capital letters in the same places? If they are different, why?*

Session 3

Introduction

Tell the story shown in the pictures on **Copymaster 6**. Make sure the children know the story well enough to retell it. Read the vocabulary underneath.

Ask: *How could we make words to go under these pictures?*

Discuss various options such as stencils or careful writing. Lead the children to suggest word processing the text so that it is neat and easy to read.

Demonstrate how to keep typing until the two sentences for the first picture are finished. Let the word processor decide when to go onto a new line. Press *enter* twice when typing the caption for the next picture.

Activity

Using the pictures as a guide ask the children to type the caption for each one. They can then check for capital letters at the beginning of sentences and names.

Ask: *Is there a space between the writing for each of the pictures?*

Print out the text. Away from the computer cut the captions out and stick them under the correct pictures.

Key teaching point: That the *enter* key can be used both to move onto a new line, and to leave a space in text.

Plenary

Ask: *What else could the return key be used for?*

Suggestions could include lists, poems as in the previous lesson, and addresses on letters.

Follow-up activities

- Change lists separated by commas into lists going down the page

- Edit a short story to replace a character's name with their own

- Type an address for an envelope related to a topic.

Early painting activities

Reception/Year 1

Learning targets

1 ➤➤ to be able to use images to develop their ideas

2 ➤➤ to recognise that ICT can be used to create pictures

3 ➤➤ to select and use the appropriate tools

4 ➤➤ to be able to control the *pen tool* and use the *flood fill tool* to create visual effects

Before you start

Subject knowledge

In this unit the children may be having their first experience of creating pictures using a computer. It may also be their first real use of the mouse and the keyboard. If this is the case extra lessons reinforcing how to move the mouse, click the mouse button and press the keyboard may be needed. If Unit 1 has been covered they will already be familiar with the keyboard.

For session 2 prepare a simple outline picture, if possible fitting in with the current topic. Make sure that the lines have no gaps which would prevent the *flood fill tool* being used. If you have gaps, use *zoom* to spot the gap and close it. You can use the *undo tool* if the colour spills out beyond the outline. If the picture is hard to draw and you cannot scan it, trace it onto acetate and put it onto the monitor screen. You can then trace it.

Related Learning Targets units:
This unit is the first in its series. It leads to:
KS1 Unit 5 *Developing painting skills*

QCA ICT Scheme of work reference:
Leads to Unit 2B *Creating pictures*

Assessment

Can the children use the *pen tool* with care?
Can the children use the *flood fill tool*, selecting the colour required?
Can they appreciate the advantages of using a computer to create images?

Resources

Paint program
Ready prepared outline picture file prepared using a pen tool within a paint package. The picture should not be *Clip art* and must not have any gaps in the outline or the fill won't work
Copymaster 7
Copymaster 8

Vocabulary

Pen tool, flood fill tool

Teaching the sessions

Session 1   ❶ ❸

Introduction

▓ Look at **Copymaster 7**. Discuss how the picture would look better if it was coloured in.

> **Ask:** *What colours should we choose? Why have you chosen that colour?*

Look at the selection of colouring tools to be used. Decide whether to use crayons or felt tip pens.

Activity

👤 Give the children copies of Copymaster 7. Encourage them to colour the picture in, changing colours when they need to.

> **Ask:** *How can you make your picture look very neatly coloured in?*

Encourage the children to try and stay inside the clear lines when colouring.

> **Key teaching point:** That when colouring a picture we need to select the correct tools.

Plenary

As a group look at the finished pictures.

> **Ask:** *Which part of your colouring did you like best? Have you managed to stay inside the lines for most of the time?*

Session 2

Introduction

▓ The children will need an explanation of what the computer is if they have not used one before.

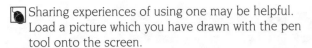 Sharing experiences of using one may be helpful. Load a picture which you have drawn with the pen tool onto the screen.

Ask: *Where did this picture come from?*

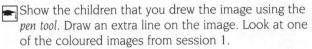 Show the children that you drew the image using the *pen tool*. Draw an extra line on the image. Look at one of the coloured images from session 1.

Ask: *What is the difference between these two pictures?*

Ask the children how the black and white image on the computer screen can be coloured in. Demonstrate how to choose a colour and how to use the *pen tool* to colour an area. Show how easy it is to go over the lines. Select the *flood fill tool*. Fill some areas in various colours. Point out how the colour does not spill over the lines. Show the children what will happen if there are gaps in the line when the *flood fill tool* is used. Demonstrate how to use the *undo tool*.

Activity

Load the image for the children. Let them select colours and use the *flood fill tool* to colour in the image. Print out the images.

Key teaching point: That the *flood fill tool* is easier to use for colouring than the *pen tool*.

Plenary

Point out that sometimes it is better to colour with crayons, and sometimes it is good to use a computer. Tell them that computer images can be printed out more than once. Show how the images coloured with crayons can be done anywhere, not just where a computer is.

Session 3

Introduction

Look at **Copymaster 8**.

Ask: *If you wanted to draw pictures like this on a computer what tool would you use? What tool would be best to use to colour them in?*

Activity

Ask the children to use the *pen tool* to draw some simple objects. Let them look at Copymaster 8 for ideas. Ask them to use the *fill tool* to colour in their images. Remind them of how to use the *undo tool* if their *flood fill* spills out of their shape.

Print out the finished images.

Key teaching point: That the pupils can create their own image by using the proper tools and thinking carefully about what they do.

Plenary

Look at the finished images.

Ask: *Which part of your pictures are you most pleased with? How did you choose the colours you used?*

Display the pictures as a class art gallery.

Follow-up activities

- Colour in a pre-prepared image of tessellating shapes to give a tile pattern.
- Repeat the colouring activity using the *flood fill tool* for other topics.
- Change the colours of an outline picture that has been *flood filled*.

Developing painting skills

Year 2

Learning targets

1 ➤➤ to be able to enter and store information in a variety of forms
2 ➤➤ to be able to select and use the *pencil tool*, *geometric shapes tool*, *flood fill* and *spray tool*
3 ➤➤ to use *save as*

Before you start

QCA ICT Scheme of work reference:
Unit 2B *Creating pictures*

Subject knowledge

To be able to produce satisfactory images using a computer the children will need to be taught to use the various tools included in a paint package. Using the *pencil tool* alone is frustrating and gives unsatisfactory results.

In Unit 4 the children will have become aware of the possibility of producing pictures using a computer. They will know how to select colours, use the *pencil tool*, and the *flood fill*. They will also be able to use the *undo tool* to remove errors.

The skill of using *save as* to rename a file or to give it a sensible name will be transferable to other software.

Related Learning Targets units:
KS1 Unit 4 *Early painting activities*
KS2 Unit 6 *Personalised calendar*

Assessment

Are the correct tools used for the various parts of the images?
Are the children able to use *undo* to remove errors?
Were the names used in *save as* chosen to explain what the files were?

Resources

Paint program
Word processor program
Saved paint file depicting image similar to that on Copymaster 10
Copymaster 9
Copymaster 10

Vocabulary

Spray tool, flood fill, line, icon, pencil tool, save as

Teaching the sessions

Session 1 ②

Introduction

▨ Look at some abstract art which uses shapes in its design. Look at the example on **Copymaster 9**.

◪ Open a paint package to draw a square using the *pencil tool*. Show how difficult it is to draw straight lines, and to make the sides all the same length. Demonstrate how to use the *geometric shapes tool* to draw shapes easily. Draw a series of shapes, some in spaces and some overlapping. Use the *flood fill* to fill shapes, part shapes and background. Revise how to use *undo* to correct errors.

Ask: *What are the shapes we can choose from with the geometric shapes tool?*

Activity

▨ Using Copymaster 9 for ideas if necessary, encourage the children to produce their own abstract work of art using the *geometric shapes tool* and the *flood fill tool*.

Key teaching point: That making good use of tools helps us to produce better images.

Plenary

◪ Demonstrate how the *geometric shapes tool* is equally suited to producing pictures of objects.

Ask: *Which shapes would we use to help us draw a car, a house or a rocket?*

Session 2 ②③

Introduction

▨ Look at **Copymaster 10** and, if possible, some images of fireworks.

Ask: *What would improve the picture on Copymaster 10?*

 Suggest, if necessary, that colour would improve it. Load the prepared outline image of fireworks into the paint program. Make the background black and the drawings white to fit the topic of fireworks. Otherwise use the *geometric shapes tool* to create a couple of fireworks. Add black speckled dots to create sparkling patterns.

Ask: *Could we colour the fireworks with the flood-fill tool? What would happen?*

Show how the *flood fill tool* would spill out from the speckled patterns depicting the firework. Try using the *pencil tool* – it does not look like fireworks. Use the *spray tool*. Change the colours and use again.

Demonstrate how to use *save as* to give the finished image a new name.

Ask: *What should we call our picture? Is that a sensible name?*

Point out that they need to be able to find the picture easily.

Activity

The children colour the picture using the *spray tool* for the fiery patterns and the *fill tool* for the cylinders of the fireworks. Use *save as* to save the finished image.

Key teaching point: That deciding which tool to use affects the finished image.

Plenary

Compare the finished images by looking at them on screen. If possible use a program to display them as a quickly prepared slide show.

Session 3 ① ③

Introduction

Open one of the children's images onto the screen. Remind them that the picture is easy to find because it was given a sensible name.

Ask: *What would make this image even better for people to appreciate?*

Explain that a title and the artist's names would make it like an image in an art gallery.

Ask: *Does anybody know how we could do this?*

If the children do not realise that they can load their own images into a document explain that it is quite easy.

Show the pupils how to insert a picture into a document. Add the title and the names of the children who drew the image. Use *save as* to give a new name to this document.

Activity

 The children work in the same pairs as in Session 2 to insert their picture into a document and add the title and their names. They then save using *save as*. Print out the finished work.

Key teaching point: Using *save as* means they can give documents sensible names.

Plenary

Explain that they are going to stick their work into a class book. This will look like the art books in the library with the picture, title and name. Look at the printouts.

Ask: *Which tools were used for which parts of the pictures?*

Follow-up activities
* Make words for signs using geometric shapes and the *flood fill* to construct large colourful letters.
* Use the *spray tool* to create a background for an image drawn with the *pencil tool*.
* Make a map of the playground using geometric shapes, the *flood fill* and the *spray tool*.

Musical composition

Year 1/2

Learning targets

1 ➡ to use a variety of ICT tools

2 ➡ to realise that ICT can be used to reorganise sounds

3 ➡ to use icons to arrange musical notes or phrases

Before you start

Subject knowledge

Software dedicated to producing musical compositions may be tailored to suit the age of the children. As in other software various levels of difficulty can be selected by choosing a colour coded user level.

Children can develop their musical skills whilst learning to interact with a different type of interface. The creative side of this activity is very fulfilling. There are links to control work because the children will give a sequence of instructions and find out what happens as a result.

Related Learning Targets units:
This unit is the first in its series. It leads to:
KS2 Unit 11 *Virtual tour of the school*

QCA ICT Scheme of work reference:
Links with Unit 1F *Understanding instructions and making things happen*

Assessment

Did the final piece of music produced show evidence of choice in all taught features? Were the children able to make the music fit a certain mood?

Resources

Musical composition program
Xylophone
Copymaster 11
Copymaster 12

Vocabulary

Icon, notes, instrument icon

Teaching the sessions

Session 1 ② ③

Introduction

▓ Look at **Copymaster 11**. Look at the first musical representation. Explain that each of these dots represents a sound made by an instrument. These are called *notes*.

Ask: *Are the notes all the same or different?*

They are different. The notes that are high up are high notes. The notes that are low down are low notes. Play a high and a low note and relate them to the notes on Copymaster 11.

Repeat with the second diagram, this time explaining that the longer the note the longer the sound being made.

▰ Load the computer program. Show the children how to drag the notes onto the staves. Put them high or low. Choose long, short or medium length notes. Demonstrate how to play the music, and how to listen to it. Show them how to change any notes which they do not like.

Activity

👥🔊 Allow the children to create and listen to their own music. Ask them to listen to what they have made, and to change it if they think it could be improved.

Key teaching point: That selecting and placing the notes makes the music.

Plenary

Discuss what they found out from their work.

Ask: *Did you like all of the music you made? Did anybody alter the music and make it better?*

Session 2 ② ③

Introduction

▓🔊 Load the computer program. Play the children some music.

▰ Show the children how to adjust the volume and the speed.

Ask: *Does it make the music different?*

▰ Show the children how to change the instrument that the music is played on. Select an instrument and ask them if they can identify it.

Activity

 Allow the children to work together to produce a piece of music with all of the features carefully selected. Remind them to listen to the music and to change it if they are not happy with the effect.

Key teaching point: That selecting different features can change the nature of the music produced.

Plenary

Select one piece of music to play.

Ask: *How does it make you feel?*

Discuss the way different volumes and speeds in music produce different feelings.

Session 3 ② ③

Introduction

Look at **Copymaster 12**. Tell the children that they are going to make some music to go with a television programme. Look closely at the picture on the TV screen.

Ask: *What does this picture make us think about? What sort of music would be best to go with this picture?*

Suggest that quick, lively music would go best with this picture.

Activity

Ask the children to produce a piece of background music for the TV programme. Ask them to think about quiet or loud parts, about the notes being long or short, the musical instrument being played. Finally remind them that they will be able to change the speed of the music.

Key teaching point: That making careful choices can produce better results.

Plenary

Ask the children to list the ways in which they could vary their music.

Ask: *Did your music fit the picture?*

Follow-up activities

• Compose music to go with a puppet show.

• Prepare some music to be loaded and to try out with different instruments.

• Listen to pieces of music with different moods.

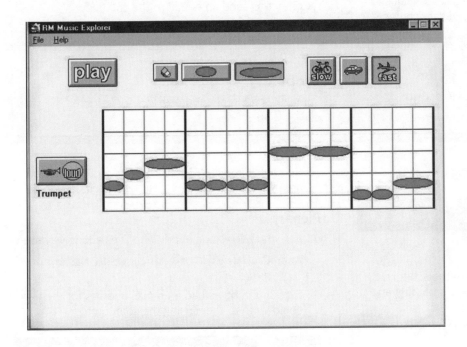

This RM *Music Explorer* (RM) screen shows the various simple features which can be used by pupils in KS1. These include different lengths of notes, different speeds, various instruments and different volumes.

E-mail introduction

Learning targets

1 ➤➤ to know about the uses of ICT inside and outside school

2 ➤➤ to know that e-mail can be used to send messages over distances

3 ➤➤ to be able to read and reply to e-mails

Before you start

Subject knowledge

The children will know that text can be entered into a computer. They will have had varying experiences of different forms of communication.

Various strategies can be used to get people to send e-mails to the children. The teacher can send an e-mail with news about school or questions on a topic. Trusted contacts could be asked to be correspondents. There are various ICT support groups who try to put schools in contact with one another for the purpose of practising e-mail skills. These should provide reliable and safe contacts for the children. Never allow pupils to send e-mails with pictures of themselves and strongly discourage use of surnames in e-mails.

Related Learning Targets units:
This unit is the first in its series. It leads to:
KS2 Unit 12 *Growing stories*

QCA ICT Scheme of work reference:
This unit leads to Unit 3E E-*mail*

Assessment

Do the children understand the advantage of using e-mail to communicate?
Can they identify an e-mail address amongst other text?
Have they an idea of how e-mails are sent and received?

Resources

E-mail program
Contact to send an e-mail to the children
Leaflets which give e-mail addresses
Copymaster 13
Copymaster 14

Vocabulary

e-mail, send, reply, address, @

Teaching the sessions

Session 1 ① ②

Introduction

Show the children an envelope with the school address and a stamp on it. Ask them what it is and what it was used for.

Ask: *Has anybody else had a message recently? How did it arrive?*

Discuss telephones, verbal messages, text messages, letters and faxes. Ask if anybody has received an e-mail. Explain what it is and how it works. Discuss the advantages and disadvantages of each form of communication.

Activity

Use **Copymaster 13** to send messages to a partner in the class. Post the message into a posting box. Empty the box, deliver the messages and read them. Use the system to send a message again to reply if time permits. Explain that this is rather like an e-mail. Discuss the advantages of being able to post a message and have it delivered quickly.

Key teaching point: Emphasise the fact that e-mails are quick and can travel great distances.

Plenary

Ask who knows somebody who lives a long way away.

Ask: *Could we give them a message like the ones written in the lesson?*

Explain that if we had an e-mail address for them we could write to them using the computer.

Session 2 ② ③

Introduction

Remind the children of the various ways of sending messages.

Ask: *Which ones would allow a message to travel quickly from a long way away? Has anybody found out more about e-mails?*

Activity

Arrange for the children to receive an e-mail. Make sure it includes questions which will need answering.

 Open and read the e-mail with them.

Ask: *Where did this message come from? How did it get to our computer?*

Explain the answers to these questions. Explain that many people use e-mails to keep in touch with friends and family who live a long way away.

Demonstrate how to reply to the e-mail. Ask the children to dictate replies to the questions on the e-mail. Type in the answers into the reply. Send the e-mail.

Ask: *How will this reply reach its destination?*

Key teaching point: That e-mails carrying messages travel over distances quickly.

Plenary

Ask for suggestions of people who the children would like to e-mail if they were able to. Emphasise that they must only use e-mail with permission from their parents, guardians or teachers. Ask them to find out whether they can send e-mails from home, or whether any adults they know use e-mail at work. Explain that the school sends and receives e-mails.

Session 3

Introduction

Look at a printout of the e-mail received during the first lesson. Fill in the e-mail address from the printout on **Copymaster 14**. Ask if anybody has found out if adults they know use e-mail. Fill in the e-mail address of the school. Fill in the survey sheet on Copymaster 14 with all of the e-mail information. Look at the different parts of the address. Look at those which have a clear indication of whose e-mail address it is. These may include parts of names of people or businesses.

Ask: *Is there a symbol which tells us that it is an e-mail address? Can we put this address on an envelope and post it?*

Activity

Ask the children to look at a variety of leaflets including those from museums, businesses, schools and theatres. Look at other sources of e-mail addresses such as posters. Remind them to search for the @. Let them enter the e-mail addresses onto the survey sheet.

Key teaching point: That many people use e-mail to communicate quickly and easily.

Plenary

Look at the addresses discovered. Do any of them have evidence of the country they are from, such as 'uk' or 'au'? What would the children choose as a fun e-mail address for themselves? Remember to discourage them from using their surnames in e-mails.

Follow-up activities

• Send e-mails to ask for information on a topic.
• Arrange to send e-mails to other classes, or work in groups to send e-mails to each other.

23

HANDLING DATA

Units 8–14

This section covers a very wide range of activities. It starts by introducing and increasing the vocabulary of sorting. It then progresses through various stages to using a database to ask and find answers to questions. This area of ICT, more than others, needs careful preparation before the lesson. The activities involved require the teacher to set up files beforehand so that the lesson is productive.

Resource Issues

Binary databases, which are covered in Unit 12, can be of varying degrees of sophistication. *Decision tree* (Flying Fox) is good for Key Stage 1 as it can make files look attractive by including pictures and coloured backgrounds. Other more basic software can still fulfil the requirements of the key stage. Making the files can be tricky at first but it is possible, and means that the work can be made to fit in with a topic. Often there are suitable files provided with the software. Programs other than specific binary database programs can be used to make a decision tree. You could produce a small website, use a *PowerPoint* presentation or use other simple multimedia packages to devise pages to form a binary database.

Drag and drop programs make sorting using the computer fun. *My World*3 has sorting activities. These could be adapted, but only with a fair amount of effort. *Textease* 2000 can also be used for dragging and dropping activities.

The ability to select different levels of difficulty in programs is particularly important in data handling. An over-complicated interface could put the children off. Specific programs should preferably be provided for Key Stage 1, which suit the requirements both of ICT and the mathematical skills involved in handling data.

Teaching Issues

In the early stages of sorting the teacher will need to make sure that the children are familiar with the objects that they are sorting. Allow them to sort carefully selected objects into groups which are already labelled with properties. They will need some practice and guidance to be able to identify their own useful properties to sort things by.

It is important, even at this stage, to analyse the findings when using graphs or databases. There is no point in even collecting data without progressing to this. This can be challenging, but the simple data required by these pupils can easily be arranged to give examples of situations which bring about learning. The main participation by the children can be on any stage of the database work, with the teacher guiding the children through the rest of the process.

It is too much to ask the children to carry out every part of the process in an independent way. Decide whether the objective is to devise a questionnaire, to collect the data, to enter the data into the database or to analyse the data. Then devise an activity which allows them to practise the skills which fit in with the objective. If the main emphasis is not on the analysis, as may happen when the children spend a lot of time on collecting data, then carry out the analysis as a class activity. Try not to miss it out, as it is the key element in the process.

Cross-curricular Links

Maths

The graphing of data can be used to help organise information. As a result of a survey charts can be used to show the maximum and minimum amounts recorded as well as to show the comparative amounts.
- Graph prices of items in a shop.
- Graph the lengths of objects measured in a lesson.

Science

Data handling can be used either to help interpret the findings of an experiment or to work on the properties of materials and living things.
- Graphs can be used to show the results of a pushing or pulling experiment.
- Living things or materials can be sorted according to their properties to help further understanding.
- A database of animals could be searched to find those that live in particular habitats.

Geography

Fieldwork linked to environmental studies may produce data that can be graphed. Studies of localities may produce information that can be entered into a database. This can then be searched and sorted.
- Search a simple database of seaside facilities.
- Graph the litter found in different parts of the playground.

PE

ICT could be used to look at data acquired during PE lessons.
- As part of work on fitness and health children could record how their bodies feel during different activities.
- Children could graph their progress in sports activities such as how many times they can catch a ball before dropping it.

RE

Data about religions and festivals can be easily analysed using ICT.
- When working on Celebrations as a topic, a record could be kept of the names, dates and traditions relating to each festival. These records could then be sorted by date, festival name, traditions and symbols.

Sorting activities

Reception

Learning targets

1 ➤➤ to find and identify features of living things, objects and events they observe

2 ➤➤ to identify key words to describe objects

3 ➤➤ to sort objects into pre-determined sets

Before you start

Subject knowledge

These activities will introduce the children to the idea that objects can have properties. They will help to build up vocabulary and lay the foundation for scientific and mathematical concepts.

Using apparatus that the children are already familiar with will make these tasks more interesting and more likely to be successful.

The software used depends on what is available. *My World* has sorting activities which could be modified to fit in with requirements. *Textease* could be used to prepare a background with circles to sort into, with *Clip art* objects placed round the edge. In both cases the children can drag and drop the objects into the required sets.

Related Learning Targets units:
This unit is the first in its series. It leads to:
KS1 Unit 9 *Introduction to classification*

Assessment

Can the children sort objects into pre-defined sets?
Are the children able to suggest properties to sort by?
Can they use drag and drop to help them in their sorting activities?

Resources

Drag and drop program with sorting files
Sorting apparatus such as farm animals, zoo animals, vehicles or a dolls' house
A picture file with outline drawings of food from a paint program
Copymaster 15
Copymaster 16

Vocabulary

sort, sets, fill tool, drag

Teaching the sessions

Session 1 ➊

Introduction

Select apparatus already used in the classroom. This could include zoo animals, farm animals, a dolls' house, or a selection of vehicles. Sort the objects into sensible sets. Farm animals can be sorted into fields and buildings, zoo animals sorted into their paddocks, vehicles sorted into the sections of a car park and house furniture sorted into the rooms of the dolls' house. Discuss reasons for putting objects in particular groups.

Ask: *Why have I put this object in this group?*

Activity

Allow the children to experiment with moving the actual objects round from group to group. Discuss with them the reasons for the groupings.

Complete **Copymaster 15**. Ask the children to match the pet with its home or bed. Use an arrow to indicate which pet goes where.

Key teaching point: To make the children aware of the fact that some objects have things in common with each other.

Plenary

Look at the answers to Copymaster 15. Ask the children to give reasons for the places they 'put' the pets.

Session 2

Introduction

The children can now use a computer to sort pictures of objects. Use a program which allows the children to drag pictures into sets. *Textease* is an ideal program for this. *My World* has some ready-to-use files. Ideas could include sorting clothes into warm and cool clothing, sorting animals into those that live on land, in the water or fly in the air, or sorting vehicles by the number of wheels they have.

Show the children how they can click on an object, hold the mouse button down, and drag the object to another place on the screen. Remind them of the previous lesson when they thought about where they might like to put objects.

Ask: *Where should we put this object?*

Activity

Encourage the children to sort the objects on the screen into the sets required. Talk to them and ask them for reasons for their sorting.

Key teaching point: That objects have properties and can be sorted by them.

Plenary

Load another sorting activity into the computer. Ask for suggestions on how to sort the objects. Discuss the ideas that the children come up with. Move the objects first into one grouping, then reorder them in another way.

Session 3

Introduction

Remind the children about the previous lessons on sorting objects. Ask the children about what things they can eat and what they cannot. Show them **Copymaster 16**.

Ask: *Which of these things can you eat?*

Explain that these objects could be sorted out into those we can eat and those we cannot.

Activity

Ask the children to colour in the things which they are allowed to eat. This will put all the coloured items into one set.

Load a file with outline drawings of edible foods. Ask the children to use the *fill tool* to colour in the food which they like to eat. Anything they do not like they should leave uncoloured. Ask the children to add their names if they are able to. Print out their finished work.

Key teaching point: That the same objects can be sorted in different ways.

Plenary

Look at the printouts of the colouring of the food. Do they vary?

Ask: *Why have Jo and Samir coloured in their pictures differently?*

Explain that different people like different things. When we sort according to likes and dislikes we may have different results.

Follow-up activities

- Sort stickers or cut-out images into sets by sticking them into labelled circles or squares.
- Sort the children into groups, by eye colour, hair colour, birthdays or some other property.
- Sort construction materials according to various properties.

Introduction to classification

Year 1

Learning targets

1 ➤➤ to be able to enter and store information in a variety of ways
2 ➤➤ to recognise that objects have properties
3 ➤➤ to be able to identify criteria which divide a set of objects
4 ➤➤ to be able to provide information about objects

Before you start

Subject knowledge

Although this unit could be completed without a computer it still teaches key ICT skills as it helps to provide the children with the skills that they will need to use databases. The activities carried out in Unit 8 are very similar, in that they give the children a chance to discuss the properties of objects. The language used in this unit should be a little more advanced than that used in Unit 8, progressing in a similar fashion to that covered in shape work in mathematics.

To develop the children's ability to suggest their own properties for sorting, start with more restricted properties and then progress to sorting items with less obvious similarities and differences.

If required, a program such as *My World* or *Textease* 2000, which allows drag and drop of objects, can be used to complete a sorting activity.

Related Learning Targets units:
KS1 Unit 8 *Sorting activities*
KS1 Unit 10 *Creating and using pictograms*
QCA ICT Scheme of work reference:
Unit 1D *Labelling and classifying*

Assessment

Can the children guess an object from its description?
Can the children suggest a method of sorting objects into two sets?
Are the pupils increasing their descriptive vocabulary?

Resources

Drag and drop program with sorting files
Sorting apparatus
Copymaster 17
Copymaster 18

Vocabulary

Information, key words, sets

Teaching the sessions

Session 1 ② ③

Introduction

Revise the use of the basic words used to describe size. Use the words 'big', 'middle-sized' and 'little'. You could also use the words 'large' and 'small'.

Demonstrate how to sort some similar objects into sets according to their relative size. If possible have objects in three sizes. Duplicate some objects so that there is more than one object that is, for instance, big. This will stop them getting too used to putting just one object into each set. Use labels such as 'little', 'middle-sized' and 'big'.

Ask: *Are any of these boxes big?*

Show the children how to use labelled hoops or shapes drawn on paper to sort the objects into.

Activity

 Use the labelled hoops or shapes drawn on paper to sort the objects into. When the children are confident with this practical activity look at the image from the Goldilocks story on **Copymaster 17**. Discuss the sizes of the objects.

Ask: *Which do you think is the big bowl?*

Look at the words on the labels. Which chair should have an arrow to the word 'big'? Complete the arrows for all of the objects, linking them either to 'big', 'middle-sized' or 'little'.

Key teaching point: Emphasise the importance of looking at more than one object before deciding on its size.

Plenary

Show the children one new object. Show them a fairly big book, but have an even bigger one in reserve.

Ask: *What size is this book?*

When they say that it is big reveal a small book and an even bigger book.

Ask: *Do you still think that this book is big?*

Discuss whether they still think the first book is big, perhaps because it would not fit in their school bag, or on their bookshelf at home. Have some of them changed their minds?

Session 2 ② ③

Introduction

 Use a set of logic materials to discuss vocabulary relevant to describing the properties of objects. If no purpose-made set is available use a set of objects of varying colours, shapes and sizes (empty cartons could be covered for this purpose). Have a similar discussion to that in Session 1.

Play a guessing game where the colour and size of an object are described and the children try to guess what the object is. If there are objects of different shapes as well the children should not have a hundred percent success rate, making them realise that the more they describe the object the more they are likely to succeed.

Ask: *It is big and green. What shape is it?*

Activity

 Use **Copymaster 18** to give practice in remembering two properties for one object. Colour in the key to the colours together to help in reading the words.

If the children are increasing in confidence allow them to play the guessing game in pairs. The children take it in turn to describe an object by its shape and colour. Let them keep score of their successes by taking a counter from a bowl each time they guess correctly. The first child to reach a score of five is the winner.

Key teaching point: That by describing the properties of objects we may be able to identify them.

Plenary

Have a final guessing game where the children try to guess which of a set of objects the teacher is thinking about. Make sure they know the colours and sizes which they can choose from.

Session 3 ① ④

Introduction

 Select a less structured set of objects to be sorted. Items such as fruit or toys could be used. Pictures of pets would also provide lots of vocabulary. Move away from the restrictions of shape, colour and size in this activity.

Ask: *Who can tell me something interesting about this?*

The range of comments is now increased. Pupils may comment on the purpose of the item, the place it is kept, its age or endless other ideas. Encourage them to think of some property which is shared by some of the other objects. In the case of fruit, it may be to say that it has to be peeled before we can eat it. With pets it may be to say that it can fly.

Activity

 Use sets of objects which give the children a chance to sort the objects by their own criteria. Encourage them to sort the objects into two sets, with the possibility of discarding a small group of objects that do not fit into any category.

Ask: *Why have you put these objects all into the same set?*

If desired this activity can also be covered using pictures of objects and a program similar to the one used in Unit 8. This time the method used for sorting should be more open-ended. Although you will have some idea of how the objects could be sorted it should be possible for the children to choose different criteria altogether.

Key teaching point: That there are many things that a set of objects could have in common.

Plenary

Show the children two sets of objects, sorted with particular criteria in mind.

Ask: *How have I sorted these objects?*

Discuss the possibilities. Make it clear that as long as they can explain their chosen criteria they cannot really be wrong. Their idea may be different from yours, but neither is more correct than the other.

Follow-up activities

• Use a computer based activity if one has not already been used.

• Make a frieze depicting a scene where objects have been sorted. Label some of the criteria.

• Use a word bank to make labels for items according to their properties.

Creating and using pictograms

Year 1/2

Learning targets

1 ➤➤ to be able to share their ideas by presenting information in a variety of forms
2 ➤➤ to recognise that there is a relationship between data collected, sorted and classified and a pictogram
3 ➤➤ to be able to enter data into a graphing package to create a pictogram

Before you start

Subject knowledge

The idea of sorting data will already have been introduced in Units 8 & 9. This unit allows the children to progress to using the computer to help analyse their data. Presenting it as a graph means that the data is easier to interpret.

Although it is easy to set up a file specifically for a topic there are often files prepared which allow data to be entered and graphed easily. These often also include *Clip art* which both helps the children to know what the text is saying and makes inputting the data a pleasant experience.

This unit describes how to progress through collecting the data, graphing the findings and then analysing what is shown by the graphs. Although it is based on a traffic survey it could easily be adapted to fit any topic. It is essential to first identify what the children want to find out. Arrange to collect data that can be compared, either by collecting data twice in the same place at different times, or by doing so in two different places. You could also conduct a survey to compare vehicle

types. This unit assumes that you will compare the numbers of each type of vehicle, but it would be easy to adapt to do another option.

Related Learning Targets units:
This unit is the first in its series. It leads to:
KS1 Unit 9 *Introduction to classification*
QCA ICT Scheme of work reference:
Unit 1E *Representing information graphically: pictograms*

Assessment

Can the children enter data from a data collection sheet accurately?
Are the children able to select the type of graph required for the data being graphed?
Are the observations made after looking at the graph reasonable?

Resources

Graphing package and prepared file for entering data into
Copymaster 19
Copymaster 20

Vocabulary

Pictogram, survey, data, graph, report

Teaching the sessions

Session 1 ②

Introduction

▦ Explain to the children that they are going to try to find out which vehicle we see most of near the school. Explain that they will be counting the various sorts of vehicles. To do this they will need a tally sheet. Look at **Copymaster 19**. Explain that they will draw a line for each vehicle they see. Show how they can use the pictures of the vehicles to help them to know where to tally.

Ask: *Which sort of vehicle do you think we will see most of? Why? Which sort of vehicle do you think we will see least? Why?*

Activity

▦ Carry out the survey from a safe vantage point. Encourage the children to work in pairs, one spotting and one tallying. Let them know when they are halfway through their survey time so that they can swap if they wish. It may be helpful to have an adult doing a tally on a separate survey sheet as a backup source of data.

Key teaching point: That they are able to collect authentic interesting data to use in their work.

Plenary

Back in school look at the completed survey sheets. Count up the totals for each type of vehicle. Explain that this will help us enter data into the computer program that will help us draw graphs.

Ask: *Has everybody got similar totals for each vehicle type? Is it easy to work out which vehicle we saw most of?*

Session 2

Introduction

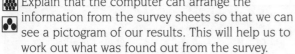 Explain that the computer can arrange the information from the survey sheets so that we can see a pictogram of our results. This will help us to work out what was found out from the survey.

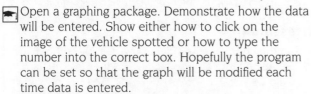 Open a graphing package. Demonstrate how the data will be entered. Show either how to click on the image of the vehicle spotted or how to type the number into the correct box. Hopefully the program can be set so that the graph will be modified each time data is entered.

Explain that we can watch our graph growing as we enter the data.

Show them the various types of graph. Ask them to choose the bar chart as this will make it easier to compare the numbers of different vehicles.

Activity

Allow the children to enter the data from their survey sheets. Encourage them to click carefully so that extra entries are not added.

Demonstrate how to correct an error if they make one.

Ask the children to save and print their graphs and write their names on them if the computer program did not ask them to do so.

Key teaching point: That the computer can draw a neat and accurate graph if we enter the data carefully.

Plenary

Compare the graphs. If there are any obvious differences look at the survey sheet to check if the data was entered correctly. Explain that we need to keep the graphs safely as we still have more work to do with them.

Session 3

Introduction

Give the children their graphs back from the previous lesson. Explain that there is no point in making a graph if we do not look closely at it to see what it tells us. Recap what the survey was meant to tell us.

Ask: *How can we tell which vehicle we saw most of? Which vehicle did we see least of? What other things might we be able to find out from our graphs?*

Discuss items such as more than one type of vehicle with the same number of observations, or vehicles that were not seen at all. Ask why certain vehicles might have been seen a lot. For instance, were they watching traffic on a bus route?

Activity

Show the children **Copymaster 20**. Explain that some of the ideas they have been discussing can be recorded on this sheet. They may use Copymaster 19 as a word bank. Read through the questions already on the report sheet.

Ask: *Which vehicle should you write here?*

Ask the children whether they have any ideas of what they could write in the blank space.

Key teaching point: That a graph makes it easy for us to compare the information for each vehicle.

Plenary

Ask the children to read out the statements on their report form. What did they choose for their own comment? Did they say how many of one vehicle they saw?

Ask: *How many of us got the same answers? Why might we have got different answers?*

Follow-up activities

• Collect data on favourite food. Ask the children to select from a limited list. Graph the data and analyse the findings.

• Count and graph the toy farm animals in the classroom.

• Graph the number of sides on a set of shapes.

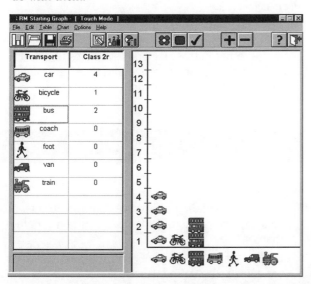

This pictogram was created using RM *Starting Graph* (RM). This standard file, provided with the software, can be adapted to suit any purpose. There are various ways of entering the data. The numbers in the chart can be altered, or the images can be clicked on to add another vehicle. Either way, the data chart and graph reflect the same data.

HANDLING DATA
UNIT 11

Sorting diagrams

Year 2

Learning targets

1 ➤➤ to be able to share their ideas by presenting information in a variety of forms

2 ➤➤ to be able to process and sort data by sorting and classifying

3 ➤➤ to describe objects from key words

Before you start

Subject knowledge

These lessons develop a slightly different sorting skill to the two previous lessons. Work on vocabulary and attributes of objects already covered will greatly help in this work. However the logic aspects of this work will help when other database work is completed in Key Stage 2. The pupils will learn how a single object can belong to two different sets when sorting objects. It will also become clear that some objects do not belong in either of the sets designated.

Copymaster 21 will need the sets labelling before photocopying. For Session 3 either have the images for the children ready to load, or, if they are able to insert pictures themselves, allow them to find their own pictures.

Related Learning Targets units:
KS1 Unit 10 *Creating and using pictograms*

QCA ICT Scheme of work reference:
Builds on Unit 1C *The information around us* and Unit 1E *Representing information graphically: pictograms*

Assessment

Can the children sort objects by their properties?
Are the children able to suggest properties which would be suitable for sorting?
Did the children use the software satisfactorily to present their sorted objects?

Resources

Sorting hoops and labels
Objects to sort
Drag and Drop program
Copymaster 21
Copymaster 22

Vocabulary

Sets, properties, overlay, drag and drop

Teaching the sessions

Session 1 ②③

Introduction

Revise the idea of describing properties of objects. Sort some buttons into sets. Allocate a new set for each new property. Look at the array of sets. Move one or two buttons into different sets. For example, move a white button from the white set into the set with two holes.

Ask: *Which set should this button really be in?*

Explain that it should really be in both sets. Arrange the hoops so that they overlap. Sort the buttons into the two sets, including placing those belonging in both sets into the overlapping area. The hoops could be labelled 'white buttons' and 'buttons with two holes'. Place buttons which fit in neither set outside the hoops.

Activity

Allow the children to finish sorting the buttons. Record their findings on the blank Venn diagram on

Copymaster 21. Remind them that some buttons will not go into either of the sets.

Encourage the children to discuss their work as they sort the buttons.

Key teaching point: That objects can have more than one property, and thus belong in two sets.

Plenary

Hold up a button. Ask the children to suggest as many properties of the button as possible. Repeat with another button. Include references to colour, size, number of holes, shape and thickness. Label the new sets. Ask the children to sort the buttons into these sets.

Session 2 ②

Introduction

Remind the children of how we can sort objects into sets and how some objects need to go into more than one set.

Look at a series of pictures on the computer which are going to be sorted. Have them ready pasted into a file of a drag and drop program with overlapping labelled set circles already drawn on it. Look at the properties of the pictures. Discuss these.

Ask: *Can you think of a word that would describe this group of objects? What two properties might we sort these objects by?*

Show the children how to drag and drop pictures. Explain that they are going to sort the pictures in the same way that they sorted the buttons in the previous lesson. Read the labels on the sets again.

Activity

Ask the children to sort the pictures into the correct set circles. Remind them that pictures which will go in neither circle go outside the circles. Allow them to print out their completed sets.

Key teaching point: That objects can be sorted by properties.

Plenary

Look at the printouts from the activity.

Ask: *Are all the sets the same?*

Session 3 ① ②

Introduction

Cover up the labels on **Copymaster 22** and show the pictures to the children. Discuss what might be on the labels for the sets.

Ask: *What two properties would not work?*

Explain that if one circle said two legs and one said four legs, nothing would be able to go in the middle section, because nothing could have both two legs and four legs.

Activity

Complete Copymaster 22, which asks the children to sort a group of animals in two different ways.

On the computer use a similar diagram, with two sections and two overlapping circles on each. Ask the children to sort a set of pictures in two different ways and label their circles with the properties used.

Save and print out the finished work.

Key teaching point: To identify properties and sort by them.

Plenary

Ask children to stand up and explain why they have sorted the pictures as they have. See if the rest of the children agree.

Ask: *Would you have sorted these pictures in a different way?*

Follow-up activities

• Use in maths work for properties of shape.

• Work on Carroll diagrams, which also consider the shared properties of objects.

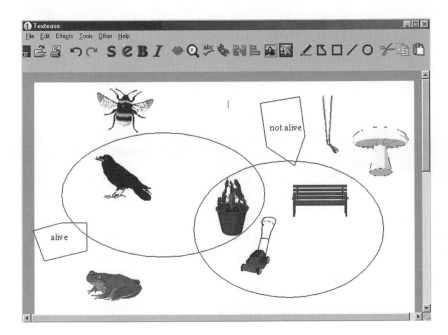

This file has been created in *Textease* 2000 (Softease). The pupils can drag and drop the pictures into the right circles. The houseplant would be in the overlap section, as it has both 'alive' and 'not alive' properties.

Binary databases

Year 1/2

Learning targets

1 ➤➤ to be able to ask questions that comply with the rule that it can only have a 'yes' or 'no' answer

2 ➤➤ to use a prepared file to identify objects

3 ➤➤ to know that the program constructs a binary tree

Before you start

Subject knowledge

This specific type of database is important in helping children to develop a system for identifying things. Asking questions and working out the answers moves them closer to knowing what something is. This leads eventually to high level skills which will help them particularly in science and maths.

Previous work on characteristics of objects will be important to this activity. If the children are not aware that objects have properties they will need to go back and do some of the sorting activities.

Prepare more than one database. Some children will find the activity difficult and will need a binary tree with only two layers of questions. Others might need the challenge of more objects and more questions.

Related Learning Targets units:
This unit is the first in its series. It links with:
KS1 Unit 9 *Introduction to classification* and Unit 11 *Sorting diagrams*
QCA ICT Scheme of work reference:
Unit 4E *Modelling effects on screen*

Assessment

Can the children make up questions about objects that have a 'yes' or 'no' answer?
Did the children manage to identify the unknown objects using the binary database?
Can the children carry out a similar process using practical activities?

Resources

Binary database with prepared files
Copymaster 23
Copymaster 24

Vocabulary

Database, yes/no question, property

Teaching the sessions

Session 1 ①

Introduction

Place a set of objects onto a tray. Tell the children that you are thinking of one of the objects. Allow them ten questions to try to work out which object you are thinking of. Explain that you must be able to answer 'yes' or 'no' to the questions. They must not guess the object until they are absolutely certain of the answer.

Ask them to try again. This time encourage them to ask questions which will divide the group of objects almost in two. Discard objects to which the answer is 'no' so that they can see the number of objects to choose from getting smaller and smaller.

Allow a child to be the person who thinks of an object. Encourage the other children to ask questions. Remove the objects with 'no' answers for the child.

Ask: *Which questions were the best for removing half of the objects?*

Activity

Introduce the idea of a simple key as a diagram. Use an enlarged version of **Copymaster 24**, filled in with questions to suit a group of objects. Move the objects down the tracks, according to the answers to the questions. At the end of the track should be the name of the object.

Ask: *How did we find out what this was?*

Use **Copymaster 23** to identify a set of minibeasts. Explain that although they might not know what the creature is called, they can find out if they use the branching database. Ask them to write the names of the creatures under each picture.

Key teaching point: That by asking a series of questions we can identify objects.

Plenary

Hold up enlarged pictures of the creatures.

Ask: *What is this creature called? How did you find out? Can you think of anything else we could make a branching database for?*

Session 2 ② ③

Introduction

Prepare Copymaster 24 with a new set of questions. Use it to identify the objects which go with it. Explain that they can use a computer program to ask the questions and to lead them to answers at the end. All they will need to do is answer 'yes' or 'no' to each question.

Load a pre-configured file into the binary database. Demonstrate how to answer the questions and what will happen when all the questions have been answered. This will vary from program to program.

Activity

Load the file that they are going to use. If possible give them pictures of the relevant objects or the objects themselves. Ask if they know what the objects are. Tell them that if they answer the questions with 'yes' or 'no' the program will tell them the answer.

Key teaching point: That a computer can be programmed to help identify objects more efficiently.

Plenary

Ask: *How did you find out what the objects were?*

Allow the children to explain the process which helped them to identify the objects.

Ask: *How did the computer know about those objects?*

Explain that this program can only work if somebody knows about the things being identified. Somebody has to enter the data and save it. If they type it in incorrectly it will give the wrong answer.

Follow-up activities

- Repeat the activity with different files. Try to use real objects which may be unfamiliar to them.

- Complete practical activities sorting objects along tracks with questions at the junctions.

- Let the children try to make up questions to sort four objects.

Searching and sorting

Year 2

Learning targets

1 ➤➤ to be able to select from and add to data they have retrieved for a particular purpose

2 ➤➤ to know that a database provides a means of storing information and can be searched

3 ➤➤ to use the *search* and *sort* tools on a simple database to find answers to specific questions

Before you start

Subject knowledge

This unit builds on all the previous work done in the Handling Data section. Although the main unit which precedes it is the one on creating pictograms other work on properties of objects is also relevant. This unit formally introduces the children to databases. After this work you should emphasise how powerful a database is for sorting information.

Before the lesson the shapes on Copymaster 25 could be enlarged. If Copymaster 25 was copied onto card it would make the task easier.

Related Learning Targets units:
KS1 Unit 10 *Creating and using pictograms*
KS2 Unit 15 *Asking questions about the wives of Henry VIII*

QCA ICT Scheme of work reference:
Unit 4E *Modelling effects on screen*

Assessment

Can the children suggest appropriate questions to use for searching?
Did the children search the database successfully?

Resources

A simple database with data entered into a file
Pieces of dowelling 15cm long
Copymaster 25
Copymaster 26

Vocabulary

data, record, field, sort

Teaching the sessions

Session 1 ② ③

Introduction

▓ Introduce the children to the idea of *records* and *fields*. Explain that each item in a database is a *record*. In the case of a database on birds each bird will have its own *record*. Each individual piece of information gathered for each *record* is called a *field*. In a bird database, fields might include colour, beak shape and size.

Ask: *What might you want to know about shapes?*

Explain that they are going to record data about a particular set of objects. Use **Copymaster 25** to prepare a set of punch cards for some shapes. Look at the pictures of the shapes.

Ask: *What properties could you sort these shapes by?*

The holes in the cards need to be punched by an adult. The children can then prepare the punch cards for sorting the shapes. Instruct them to cut a slot from the edge to the hole if the answer to a question is 'yes'.

Activity

 Show the children how to use the punch cards for answering questions. Place the cards in a bundle and orientate the trimmed corner so that all of the cards match. Decide on a question with a 'yes'/'no' answer.

Ask: *How can we quickly find all the shapes with curved edges?*

Show them how to thread the cards onto the dowelling through the hole for that question. Gently tap the cards and watch all the cards with the cut slots fall to the table. Check them with the children. They fell out because they had been allocated a yes answer by cutting a slot.

Give the children a set of questions to answer using their dowelling and cards. Make sure that all of the questions can be answered.

Key teaching point: That by entering the information onto the cards 'yes'/ 'no' questions can be answered very quickly.

Plenary

Ask the children to sit in their groups with their cards and dowelling.

Ask: *Find out quickly, using your cards, which shape is called a pentagon.*

The children will discover that unique properties are harder to sort by. Tell them how many holes and slots there would need to be if there was a card for each child. These cards can only work for fields with just a few answers and it is best with 'yes'/ 'no' questions.

 Session 2

Introduction

Explain to the children that they are going to use a new set of data punch cards. This time they are going to discuss what questions they would like to put onto the cards. Decide upon a set of objects that have data which would good to be interrogate.

Ask: *What do you think would be a good question to include?*

Accept questions which need 'yes'/ 'no' answers. Include those which have a choice of two or three answers, but point out that there would not be room for many of those on a punch card.

Ask: *What do you think would not be a good question to include?*

Guide the children towards those questions which have unique answers, such as names. Accept those questions which have too many answers to have holes and slots for all of them on a punch card.

Show the children how a second search could be made of the cards to find the shapes with the same two properties. Search for those with no curved sides, then those which have four sides. This should produce the square and oblong.

Activity

Prepare the cards shown on **Copymaster 26** either as a class, or in groups.

Allow the children to enter the data onto the cards in the same way as in Session 1. Ask them to search the cards to find answers to a set of questions.

Include one question where they are asked to search the cards, then search the cards with a 'yes' answer again.

Key teaching point: That some questions can be answered quickly by using a punch card database, but some cannot.

Plenary

Ask some children to demonstrate how they found the answers to some of their questions.

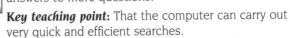 **Session 3**

Introduction

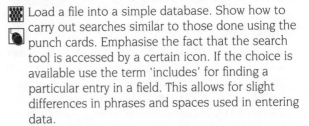 Load a file into a simple database. Show how to carry out searches similar to those done using the punch cards. Emphasise the fact that the search tool is accessed by a certain icon. If the choice is available use the term 'includes' for finding a particular entry in a field. This allows for slight differences in phrases and spaces used in entering data.

Ask: *How can I find all of the children with blue eyes?*

Show the children how to view the results if they do not appear automatically on the screen.

Activity

Allow the children to search the database for the answers to more questions.

Key teaching point: That the computer can carry out very quick and efficient searches.

Plenary

Using the same database search for an answer that would have been difficult using the punch card database. Search on a field containing a unique answer, such as a name. Show how the computer is able to do these more difficult searches easily.

Ask: *What other searches would be very easy using the computer?*

Show the children how to sort the data into alphabetical order by any field. Discuss when this might be difficult.

Follow-up activities

- Repeat the activities using information from different topics.
- Provide an activity for sorting the data. Making an index for a book would use this function.

Graphing data

Year 2

Learning targets

1 ➤➤ to be able to present information in a variety of ways

2 ➤➤ to use a computer to construct graphs

3 ➤➤ to investigate different types of graphs

Before you start

Subject knowledge

This builds on the work done in Unit 10 *Creating and using pictograms*. After producing a graph the children can consider the questions which can and cannot be answered by looking at the graph. Pupils are also required to think about which type of graph is best for the data they are graphing. The most useful graph will be the one that aids the interpretation of the data best.

The teacher will need to arrange to use data already collected. Copymaster 27 can be prepared for graphing the data by adding labels if required. More than one graph template can be prepared so that pupils can work on graphing different data.

Related Learning Targets units:
KS1 Unit 10 *Creating and using pictograms*

QCA ICT Scheme of work reference:
Unit 2E *Questions and answers*

Assessment

Can the children name the two ways they could display data in charts?
Were the children able to use a computer to draw the graphs?
Did the children express a preference for one method of producing a graph?

Resources

Database, spreadsheet or graphing program
Prepared data for graphing
Copymaster 27
Copymaster 28

Vocabulary

Information, graph, chart, bar chart, pie chart

Teaching the sessions

Session 1 ①

Introduction

▨ Look at the selected data with the children. Ask them which items of data will benefit from being graphed.

Ask: *Can we easily understand the data when it is written as a list? Would it be better if it looked more like a picture, presented on a graph?*

Activity

👤 Provide more than one set of data so that the children can work on different graphs. Some children could be graphing favourite sweets, whilst others graph favourite fruit. Provide the children with the data to be graphed and the prepared **Copymaster 27**. Ask the children to graph the data. They should then be able to answer a list of questions about the largest quantity, smallest quantity etc.

Key teaching point: That when data is graphed it can be easier to compare variables.

Plenary

Ask a representative from each group to show their graphs. Ask them to point out the interesting facts which can be seen on the graph.

Ask: *What was the largest number you had to graph? Were there any zeros in your data? How many entries had the same number?*

Session 2 ① ③

Introduction

▨ Tell the children that they are going to make a
◆ different sort of graph. Ask them how many pieces an apple pie would have to be cut into to give a piece to each member of their family. If one family cuts the pie into four and another cuts it into six, which family child would get the bigger piece? If one cake was cut into eight and another cake cut into six, which cake would have smaller pieces?

Ask: *The graph we are using today is going be like a pie cut into pieces. Some pieces will be bigger than others, some might be the same.*

Explain that the same information that was graphed in session 1 could be graphed in this different way.

Activity

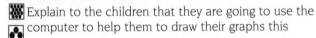 Collect data about the children. Offer six different fruits. Allow each child to choose a favourite from amongst them. Put them into groups according to which fruit they select as their favourite. Arrange each group as the section of a circle. Sit the children down in this circle. Use skipping ropes to demarcate the various sections of the pie chart formed by the different groups. Label each section.

Help the children to use **Copymaster 28** to draw this data as a pie chart.

Key teaching point: That more than one type of graph can be used to represent data.

Plenary

Show the children some more prepared pie charts. Ask them questions about the data. Look at their graphs from Session 1 and Session 2.

Ask: *Which graph is easier to understand? Which graph was easier to draw?*

Session 3

Introduction

Explain to the children that they are going to use the computer to help them to draw their graphs this

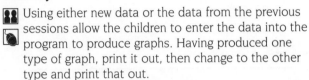 time. Load up a file that you have prepared which is ready to have the data entered. Enter the data and, if the program permits, allow the children to see the graph grow as the data is entered. Show the children how to switch between a bar chart and a pie chart.

Ask: *Which one makes this information easier to understand?*

Activity

 Using either new data or the data from the previous sessions allow the children to enter the data into the program to produce graphs. Having produced one type of graph, print it out, then change to the other type and print that out.

Key teaching point: That producing a graph using a computer is easy, neat and flexible.

Plenary

Ask the children which of the three sessions was most useful for producing useful graphs.

Ask: *Which way would you draw a chart if you had to give a copy to everybody in the class?*

Follow-up activities

• Repeat the activities using other data.

• Make a bar chart using the children themselves to represent the data.

• Answer questions from graphs not constructed by the children.

MODELLING AND CONTROL

Units 15–22

The work in this section contains activities which are sure to captivate children. The practical work using the floor robots builds on their own experience with remote controlled toys. It also is one of the best ways of giving children the chance to try out ideas and modify them according to what they observe. The *Logo* work and simulation and adventure work also may be building on their home experience. If they have access to computer games they will enjoy working out routes and trying out actions to see what effects they produce.

You may be much less familiar with this material than the children, and this may feel like a more alien sort of environment to work in. Despite this, it is hard to dispute the educational advantages of the activities, and the benefits they will give to the children's general development and thinking skills. The activities will also assist their progress in ICT.

The final unit in this section gives an opportunity to formalise the children's knowledge of the use of ICT in their surroundings.

Resource Issues

When considering which floor robot to buy it is important to investigate each one. Although some may have more features, they may be too difficult for use with younger pupils. Some have basic directional keys, others need the direction and quantity to be input. Such is the rate of progress of children of this age that both might be needed at Key Stage 1. If pupils are likely to be confident enough to try out the *repeat* function on a floor robot this feature must be available on the equipment chosen.

There is a range of software available for use with *Logo* work. The best will allow a background to be loaded for use as a maze or track for pupils to follow. Most versions will allow the pen to be lifted and dropped, which is an important feature. In a similar way to the floor robots, it is good to have a version for younger pupils where the direction keys do not require a number input. By Year 2 the children should be confident enough to use a version of *Logo* where they input a direction and a unit to say how far in that direction they want the robot to move. The ability to build procedures (a saved list of commands) is also important by Year 2. Previous to this children have been typing in commands in immediate mode.

When teaching work on adventures and simulations there is much that can be taught by using a paint package and *My World*3. The activities in these units make use of these. However, a little research will show that there are excellent simulations available for young children. For a small price the school could be equipped with a simulation for each year group. The package mentioned in Units 20 and 21 would provide an adventure for Year 1 children and another for Year 2. Searching the World Wide Web may also bring up other free adventures that can be used.

Teaching Issues

When using a floor robot there may be a problem with the amount of room needed. Some floor robots are set to a large unit of measurement as a default. It is worth investigating whether this can be reset, so that the units are smaller making the activity take up less room.

When using *Logo*, if a background can be loaded the *Logo* work can be made to fit in with a topic more easily. This makes it more stimulating for the children and makes the task more authentic.

Work in Units 20 and 21 enables the children to get the most out of their adventures and simulations. It is important that the children should be made aware of the fact that their choices bring about different results. This can be aided by using the worksheets provided with the units.

Cross-curricular Links

English

Many simulations tell a story and use the skills also covered in literacy.
- Write an account of a journey undertaken as part of an adventure. Include directional words to help explain what the journey was like.
- Write a list of words to help put together a background location for a simulation.

Maths

Although shape work is the obvious element which fits in with this there are also elements of measurement in this section.
- Draw shapes using *Logo*. Discuss the properties of the shapes and how they might be drawn by the screen turtle (or floor robot).

Design and Technology

Elements of designing and making fit in well with this topic. It also gives scope for making a design suitable for a purpose, and evaluating the design.
- Make suitable costumes for the floor robot to 'wear' when going on a journey.
- Make a large map for the floor robot to navigate.

History

Simulations are often set in historic settings and can be an excellent stimulus for discussion.
- Use an adventure set in a different time and/or location. Make notes of the main similarities and differences.
- Design a simulation to fit in with a history topic, such as *Homes Through the Ages*.

Geography

Mapwork is an obvious link with geography and simulations, however there is also scope to explore natural and man-made geographical features.
- Use of a map when using an adventure gives the children a chance to think about direction and sequence of places without even leaving the classroom.
- Make a note of the things passed in a simulation. If possible sort them into man-made and natural.

PE

The hall or playground are excellent places to develop work in Control Technology.
- Use activities in the hall to help to reinforce the directional commands needed for this work. If this can also include sequences of commands, the skills needed for control work will be developed.
- Link a series of games activities into a skills trail. Put direction cards after each activity to direct them to the next task. Tasks could include skipping, passing through a hoop etc.

PSHE

Representations in simulations and the mazes on *Logo* activities could relate to this subject area.
- Make a representation of a good place for children to get exercise, such as a playground.
- Make a *Logo* maze to find the healthy foods in a supermarket.

Using a floor robot

Reception

Learning targets

1 ➤➤ to use information technology and programmable toys to support their learning

2 ➤➤ to recognise that some machines and devices have to be controlled

3 ➤➤ to begin to put instructions in the correct sequence to achieve the correct results

Before you start

Subject knowledge

This is the first in a series of linked units. The children are likely to need basic input on the language linked to movement. They will need to work in immediate mode, not being expected to predict more than a single move of a remote controlled toy. The vehicle should be chosen for its simple controls. This should lead to the children being able to move a floor robot along a straight route.

Because of the need for resources this unit is more likely to be covered in small groups. This will also facilitate discussion of what is happening, and the use of correct vocabulary.

Related Learning Targets units:
This unit is the first in its series. It leads to:
KS1 Unit 16 *Giving instructions*

QCA ICT Scheme of work reference:
Leads to Unit 1F *Understanding instructions and making things happen*

Assessment

Do the children understand that people can control devices?
Are the children able to use simple commands to control vehicles and robots?

Resources

Simple remote controlled toy
Floor robot
Playmat or map
Copymaster 29
Copymaster 30

Vocabulary

Instruction, command, forward, backward, turn, robot

Teaching the sessions

Session 1 ②

Introduction

▓ Hold up a toy car. Ask the children who makes the car go.

Ask: *Who drives the car to the shops or to school?*

Look at **Copymaster 29**. Which of these needs somebody to make it go? Share answers. Draw circles round those selected as being controlled. Introduce the remote controlled toy. Ask if anybody knows how to make it move.

🚙 Show how to move it forwards, backwards, and how to turn it. Use the words 'forward' and 'back'.

Ask: *Which way is it going now?*

Activity

👥 Allow the children to work in pairs to move the vehicle. Encourage them to discuss which way to go next, using the correct vocabulary.

Key teaching point: That some machines can be controlled.

Plenary

Ask the children if they managed to make the vehicle move.

Ask: *What other machines can you control? Do you know how to play a video? How do we turn the lights on in the classroom?*

Encourage the children to think of other things that people control.

Session 2

Introduction

▓ Look at a playmat. Discuss the different places represented on it. Place a toy car on the playmat. (Use any other object as required.)

Ask: *How can we move the car to another place?*

🚙 Move the car along a route. Speak as you move the car along the roads. Use words such as 'forward', 'turn', 'go' and 'stop'. Demonstrate a couple of routes, asking for suggestions as to which way to go.

Activity

Ask the children to take turns at moving the car from one place to another. Encourage them to explain the directions for moving the object.

Look at **Copymaster 30**. Give each child a route to mark onto the map. Watch them as they explain the route they are taking.

Key teaching point: That routes are planned using commands such as 'forward', 'turn', 'stop' and 'go'.

Plenary

Ask the children to explain their routes, explaining why they went a particular way.

Session 3   ② ③

Introduction

Ask the children if they remember controlling the remote controlled toy, and if they remember moving the car along the route on the playmat.

Ask: *Here is a robot waiting for you to tell it where to go.*

Show how to move the floor robot from one place to another. Point the robot in the correct direction. Use the basic *forward* control. Press it once to move

forward one unit. Press it again if it has not reached its objective.

Activity

Encourage the children to 'point' the robot at a destination and use the *forward* command to move it closer and closer to the objective. Discuss the progress of the robot.

Ask: *Is the robot getting closer?*

Key teaching point: That getting the robot to its destination needs careful control of the commands.

Plenary

When all the children have had a turn gather to discuss what they have learnt.

Ask: *Did everybody manage to move the robot from one place to another? Did anybody go too far? What could you have done?*

Show the children how to use the *backward* command.

Follow-up activities

- If the robot can hold a pen try to make it draw a line to match a length of ribbon laid out on paper.
- Make a tunnel from a box and try to direct the robot through the tunnel.
- Take turns to play a short video using the 'play' and 'stop' buttons on the remote control.

Giving instructions

Year 1

Learning targets

1 ➡ to be able to plan and give instructions to make things happen

2 ➡ to recognise the importance of uniformity of instructions and measurement

3 ➡ to be able to predict the outcome of a set of instructions and test the result

Before you start

Subject knowledge

Previous work in Unit 15 covered very basic commands and the notion that machines can be controlled. The work in this unit moves on to the next stage, but will still involve work on the correct vocabulary. The children will need to become familiar with the terms right and left, although these may be represented by explicit symbols on the floor robot.

As in the previous unit the practical activities are very important in helping children to understand how to give directions in the correct order.

Session 2 could take place in the hall or on the playground, with a set of objects for starting positions and destination. Otherwise the classroom vicinity may be suitable in some schools.

Related Learning Targets units:
KS1 Unit 15 *Using a floor robot*
KS1 Unit 17 *Programming a floor robot*
QCA ICT Scheme of work reference:
Unit 1F *Understanding instructions and making things happen*

Assessment

Are the children able to use standard terms to describe routes?
When the commands are incorrect can the children identify which command needs changing?

Resources

Floor robot
Copymaster 31 (made up into sets of cards)
Copymaster 32

Vocabulary

Commands, program, floor robot, route, instruction

Teaching the sessions

Session 1　①

Introduction

Ask: *How do we know where to go when we go on a journey? Do we know what we will see on our journey? What do you see on the way to school?*

Write a few of the children's answers down or draw pictures of them, for future reference. Have they ever seen a map being used on a journey? This also lists places on the way to our holidays or to visit family.

Ask: *Do you think you could plan a route?*

Explain that the things we see on a journey could be written down in the correct order. This would help other people to find their way. This is called a route.

Activity

Ask the children to record a route using some of the pictures and symbols prepared in the Introduction. Each partner should then try to describe the other

child's route, by looking carefully at what has been drawn in the boxes.

Key teaching point: That routes can be described for somebody else to follow.

Plenary

Describe a route in the classroom. Draw it using words, pictures and symbols. Ask for a volunteer to try and describe the route you have drawn.

Ask: *Can anybody describe any part of the journey differently? Have we got anything near our school that would help a visitor to know that the school was nearby?*

Session 2　① ②

Introduction

Ask: *How do we find our way round school?*

Ask the children to direct you to a nearby location. Tell them they are not allowed to point. Point out any missing steps in their description. Explain that they must imagine that the person they are directing does not know the school at all.

Ask for a volunteer for you to direct to a visible location. Ask the children to try and guess where the child is being sent when they have enough clues. Use words such as 'forward', 'turn right', 'turn left'. If possible use a unit of measurement for the forward movements, perhaps using footsteps. For the terms 'right' and 'left' suggest, and practise, 90 degree turns as a simple standard unit.

Show the direction cards made from **Copymaster 31**. Explain that these are very clear directions that everybody understands. Remind them that they will need to include a number of steps so that people do not get lost.

Activity

Allow the children to work in pairs to plan a route from one nearby location to another. Use the cards as prompts for useful terms to use. Fill in the starting point card. Fill in the destination card but do not include it in the bundle of instructions.

When the routes are complete allow pairs of children to try out other children's routes and see if they reach the correct destination.

Key teaching point: That instructions need to be clear, precise and in the correct order.

Plenary

Ask: *Did the children discover any errors in the routes? Were the routes easy to understand?*

Ask the children to share their experiences. Explain that routes to holiday places and to visit friends and family are worked out in a similarly careful way.

Session 3

Introduction

Look at the floor robot. Explain that this is a robot which likes to obey instructions. Explain that it will do exactly what it is told to do but that we need to use instructions it understands.

Try out each of the main control buttons one by one and work out what they do. Use *forward*, *backward*, *right* and *left*. If necessary use a number to indicate

the required unit of measurement. Show how the floor robot remembers the last commands entered, unless the memory is cleared. Build up a sequence of commands, explaining that the last command is added onto the end of the previous commands. Set the robot off, and ask the children to predict where it is going to move. They should be able to remember three to four commands easily.

Ask: *How could we send the floor robot on a journey along a route?*

Remind the children that they could add one command at a time, putting the floor robot back to the start each time.

Activity

Ask the children to program a route into the floor robot to get from a starting point to a destination. Mark out the start and the destination, indicating at the start which way the floor robot is pointing. Explain that they do not need to work out the route in one go. They can program one section and try it out. Ask them to record their commands on **Copymaster 32**. This will help if they need to change anything, or to start again. They can then add the next part of the route and try it out again from the start.

Key teaching point: That if commands are put into the correct sequence they can direct a floor robot along a route.

Plenary

Try out a couple of the written procedures. Program the floor robot and place it on the start position. Set it going and see if it reaches its destination.

Ask: *What was the first command that the floor robot carried out? If a robot did not reach its destination, at what point did it go wrong?*

Follow-up activities
- If possible attach a pen and allow the robot to draw a shape.
- Make a very simple maze for the floor robot to navigate.
- Dress up the floor robot to fit in with a topic and plan a route for it.

Programming a floor robot

Year 2

Learning targets

1 ➤➤ to be able to describe the effects of their actions

2 ➤➤ to be able to predict the outcome of a set of instructions and test their prediction by programming the floor robot

3 ➤➤ to recognise that instructions can be repeated

Before you start

Subject knowledge

If the children have been able to complete Units 15 and 16 they should be well prepared to work on this unit. However, some of the concepts are very different to those they encounter in everyday life so they may still need reinforcement of vocabulary and the techniques of entering instruction into the floor robot.

Related Learning Targets units:
KS1 Unit 16 *Giving instructions*
KS2 Unit 25 *Exploring Logo*
QCA ICT Scheme of work reference:
Unit 2D *Routes: controlling a floor robot*

Assessment

Are the instructions given accurate?
Can they spot errors in their programming?
Can the children use the repeat command to produce a regular sequence of movements?

Resources

Floor robot
Copymaster 33
Copymaster 34

Vocabulary

Floor robot, commands, repeat

Teaching the sessions

Session 1 ②

Introduction

▨ Revise the need for a common language when programming the floor robot. Explain that this would still be the same if giving instructions to a person.

Ask: *What instruction do we need to include as well as the direction the floor robot is going to travel in?*

Remind the children that they need a number to say how many 'steps' forward the floor robot must go.

Activity

▨▨ Ask the children to use **Copymaster 33** to work out a sequence of instructions to move a counter round the grid, navigating around any obstacles. They should write on the command sheet and include the starting square and the finishing square. Once happy with the commands, they may cut off the instructions ready to read them out to a partner. They should read out the instructions and see if their partner agrees with the final destination of the

counter. If there is a difference the children should try to work out together where one of them made an incorrect move.

Allow the other partner to read out the instructions for moving the counter.

Key teaching point: That instructions must be given and followed with great care.

Plenary

Ask: *Who had written instructions that a partner could follow, and which led to the intended destination? Which instructions were hardest to describe?*

Session 2 ❶

Introduction

▨ Remind the children how they planned a route using the grid and counter with Copymaster 33. This time they are going to plan a route and program it into the floor robot. Revise the commands that they will need to use, and look at the buttons on the floor robot which enter these commands. Encourage the children to include the *backward* command in this activity.

Explain that the squares on the paper represent one unit of movement for the floor robot. Ask them to plan a route which changes direction often and is quite complicated. Tell them that, for this activity, they must return the floor robot to the exact position it started out from.

Show them how programming a simple oblong will bring the floor robot back to its original position. Demonstrate how to use the grid of **Copymaster 34**. Explain that you are hoping that by working out directions on the grid, they will be able to produce something much more interesting.

Activity

Allow the children to prepare their route using Copymaster 34. They can then program the directions into the floor robot. When they try it out, if it is practical the children could use a pen and allow the floor robot to trace the pattern on paper.

Key teaching point: That commands can be planned and tested.

Plenary

If the floor robot's route was marked onto paper, compare the route with the one on the grid plan.

Ask: *Are they similar? Why is one bigger than the other?*

Explain that one square on the Copymaster is much smaller than one unit of measurement by the floor robot. The floor robot enlarges the design.

Session 3

Introduction

Show the children how to use the *repeat* command.

Ask: *Why is it useful to be able to repeat a series of commands?*

Demonstrate how to enter a sequence of commands and then have them repeated. Make a small alteration to the sequence of commands and repeat them. Observe the difference. Point out that it is best, to start with, to only enter about three commands before having them repeated.

Activity

Allow the children to experiment with the *repeat* command. If possible, when an interesting program is discovered, allow the children to use a pen to record the movements on paper.

Key teaching point: That using *repeat* can save typing and produce interesting results.

Plenary

Look at some of the designs produced by using the *repeat* command.

Ask: *Can the children work out the commands used? Have any of the designs produced shapes we can name?*

Follow-up activities

- Repeat the route from Copymaster 34, but double the units for the forward or backward movements.

- Draw regular shapes by using *repeat*.

- Program the floor robot to play a part in a small drama. For example, program the robot to play the part of the wolf, stopping at each of the three pigs' houses.

Introduction to Logo

Year 1

Learning targets

1 ➤➤ to be able to plan and give instructions to make things happen
2 ➤➤ to understand that the turtle can be moved on the screen
3 ➤➤ to type in commands in immediate mode
4 ➤➤ to use commands such as *pen up* and *pen down*

Before you start

Subject knowledge

Although this is the first unit which uses a screen turtle this unit is closely related to the work covered in Units 15 to 17. The concept of using commands to make things happen should already have been covered at least once. The main development in using the screen turtle is that the command *forward* actually makes the screen turtle move in the direction it is pointing. Children tend to want to use the word *up*. The activity in Session 1 may help to minimise this problem.

For Session 3 they will need some sort of a background which provides a very basic maze, and a reason for moving the screen turtle. This could be linked with a current topic.

Related Learning Targets units:
KS1 Unit 16 *Giving instructions*
KS1 Unit 19 *Drawing shapes*

QCA ICT Scheme of work reference:
Leads to Unit 4E *Modelling effects on screen*

Assessment

Are the children able to use the commands they have learnt?
Had the children an idea of the route they were planning to take?
Did they produce a route drawn by the pen?

Resources

Logo program and a prepared background activity
Copymaster 35
Copymaster 36

Vocabulary

Screen turtle, pen down, maze, route

Teaching the sessions

Session 1 ① ②

Introduction

▨ Show the children how to load the *Logo* program. Tell the children that they are going to make the little shape on the screen, called a screen turtle, draw patterns on the screen. They are going to do this by using commands that the screen turtle can understand. To get to know these commands they are going to practise by using them on a pretend screen.

Ask: *What could we say to make the screen turtle move forward?*

Ask about the commands for backward, right and left. Use the terms the program they are going to use in Session 2 uses. If there is a choice of levels use the level which allows a single letter for the command, and uses *r* and *l* for 90 degree turns. Explain that to move forwards or backwards they will need to type a number. A bigger number goes further, a smaller a shorter distance.

Activity

▨▨ Give the children **Copymaster 35**. Explain that this picture represents the computer monitor, and the screen they will see when they direct the screen turtle. Ask one child to draw the route, and the other to give the commands. Encourage them to think of one square as one step for typing in forward and backward commands. See if the commands lead from the start to the destination.

Allow the children to swap over and repeat the activity. If possible ask them to use different routes.

Key teaching point: That the commands *f*, *b*, *r* and *l* can direct the screen turtle.

Plenary

Ask: *Did everybody manage to get from the start to the finish? Did you all avoid the obstacles?*

Session 2 ① ③ ④

Introduction

The children will transfer their skills from the paper based activity to the computer in this session. They will need directions particular to the version of *Logo* that they are using. They need to be working in immediate mode, where they type in a command and the screen turtle responds immediately. Show them how to make sure the pen is down so that they leave a trail which informs them and you as to how they are doing.

Demonstrate what each command causes on the screen.

Activity

Allow the children freedom to experiment with the commands they have learnt. In particular remind them that *f* takes the turtle in the direction it is pointing. Clear the screen and allow them to start again whenever they want to. If the children make good progress allow them to use **Copymaster 36** to give them ideas of challenging shapes to draw.

Print out their final route.

Key teaching point: That typing in commands makes the screen turtle move.

Plenary

Look at some of the printouts of the routes taken by the screen turtles. Ask the children to comment on them.

Ask: *Which screen turtle went close to the edge of the screen? How did the screen turtle turn this corner?*

Session 3 ① ③ ④

Introduction

Remind the children of the work they did in Session 1. They navigated a route. Load up the prepared activity, a background with a very simple maze. The start and finish need to be marked. This could involve pictures, such as home and school. Make the turns approximately 90 degrees.

Show the children how to navigate the maze, using the commands they have practised. Make sure the pen is down so that the route taken is shown.

Ask: *Is my route short or long?*

Activity

Allow the children to try to navigate the maze themselves. Monitor their progress and encourage them to use *back* if they have gone forward too far.

Key teaching point: Emphasise the importance of estimating the required distance to move forward.

Plenary

Load the blank background. Allow the children to enter a command one at a time. Together observe the progress towards the goal.

Ask: *How far forward do you think the screen turtle needs to go? Do we need to turn right or left?*

Follow-up activities

- Repeat the activities above using different backgrounds, and mazes of different levels of complexity.

- Draw patterns or pictures using a variety of shapes.

49

Drawing shapes

Year 2

Learning targets

1 ➤➤ to be able to plan and give instructions to make things happen

2 ➤➤ to understand that instructions can be sequenced

3 ➤➤ to know that a group of instructions can be named

Before you start

QCA ICT Scheme of work reference:
Leads to Unit 4E *Modelling effects on screen*

Subject knowledge

This session builds on the skills learnt in the floor robot work, and in Unit 18. The concepts learnt will need constant reinforcement. There are many activities which can be used to develop Unit 18 if the children are not able to progress to the work in this unit.

There are other basic commands which the children might want to learn. Some children might make the task more interesting by going backwards.

Related Learning Targets units:
KS1 Unit 16 *Giving instructions*
KS2 Unit 25 *Exploring Logo*

Assessment

Could the children visualise the commands to draw a shape?
Were the loaded procedures all functioning?
Were the *drop pen*, *lift pen*, and *change pen colour* commands used correctly?

Resources

Logo program
Copymaster 37
Copymaster 38

Vocabulary

Drop pen, lift pen, procedure, save, load

Teaching the sessions

Session 1 ① ② ③

Introduction

▦ Introduce the *Logo* program. Revise the method used to move a screen turtle. Look at **Copymaster 37**. Discuss how to draw the shape shown on the screen. Ask the children to record the commands they need on the worksheet.

Activity

▮▮ Explain that the children are going to learn how to save a set of commands so that they can use them quickly and easily.

◧ Show the children how to enter the commands as a procedure. Explain that they will give a name to the set of commands. They will then be able to type in the name of the procedure and all of the commands will be carried out.

Ask them to build a procedure to draw the shape on Copymaster 37. Save their procedure for use again. Ask them to lift the pen, move to another space, drop the pen and run their procedure. Repeat this to make a pattern on the screen.

Key teaching point: That if a set of commands is saved they can be used easily again and again.

Plenary

Ask: *What would have made your designs more interesting?*

Suggest that changing the colour of the pen would add interest to the design. Tell them how this is done in the version of *Logo* that they are using.

Session 2 ② ③

Introduction

▦ Explain to the children that they can load the procedure they saved before. They can now use this procedure in another procedure.

◧ Load a previously saved procedure. Experiment with running the procedure, turning or moving forwards, then running the procedure again.

Ask: *If this is repeated several times what does it do?*
It makes a pattern.

Activity

▦ Show the children how to build the procedure that has just been rehearsed. This will incorporate their previous procedure. When they want the new procedure to run they simply type in the name of that procedure. They can change the colour of the pen as often as they like. Try out the procedure. Change it if necessary. Save the new procedure when they are satisfied with it.

Key teaching point: That one procedure can be used in another procedure.

Plenary

Load and run the various procedures. Compare them.

Session 3

Introduction

 Remind the children of how they planned a shape and built it into a procedure.

Ask: *What did you use that procedure for?*

Revise how they built it into another procedure.

Activity

Allow the children to use **Copymaster 38** to plan a new shape. This could be an oblong or an L shaped

 box. When they like the shape they have drawn they can build it as a procedure. This can then be incorporated into another procedure as in Session 2. Remind them that they know how to change the colour of the lines. Ask them if they will lift the pen between repeating the first procedure.

Ask the children to save the procedure.

Key teaching point: That *Logo* can produce lots of different effects.

Plenary

Look at a design.

Ask: *What would have happened if there had been a quarter turn between each procedure? How many times was the first procedure used?*

Suggest other ways of varying the procedure.

Follow-up activities

• Repeat the activities above using different shapes.

• Some children may be able to use angles other than 90 degrees. If they understand that 45 is half of 90 they could use this as a practical unit of rotation.

• Draw a shape without using *forward*, replacing it with *back*.

An introduction to modelling

Year 1

Learning targets

1 ➤➤ to try things out and explore what happens in real and imaginary situations

2 ➤➤ to understand that a computer can be used to represent real situations

3 ➤➤ to understand that they can make choices and that people make different choices for different reasons

4 ➤➤ to understand that they can use a program to create a representation of a scenario

Before you start

QCA ICT Scheme of work reference:
Unit 1A An introduction to modelling

Subject knowledge

Although this is the first unit which covers this area the children will have had experiences which contribute to this work. Every time they have seen a representation of a scene they will have experienced a basic simulation. This unit will make them think about this representation, and consider how they can make one themselves.

If it is possible for this unit to be completed after Unit 4 it will make Session 2 easier to teach, since the children will have had experience of computer painting activities.

Related Learning Targets units:
This unit is the first in its series. It leads to:
KS1 Unit 21 Adventures and simulations

Assessment

Did the children's representations show thought about how to make them realistic?
Could the children name a point at which they made a choice in their simulation?
Were the children willing to explore the simulation?

Resources

A drag and drop program such as My World3
A basic adventure program such as Teacher's Cupboard, The Apple Adventure (Sherston).
Copymaster 39
Copymaster 40

Vocabulary

Realistic, imaginary, adventure, choice

Teaching the sessions

Session 1   ②

Introduction

▦ Look at a representation of a scene on a computer.

♣ **Ask:** What is real about it and what is not?

Discuss what has been done to make it realistic. The objects are probably all drawn to scale. The representation may not be shaded to give a 3D effect.

Ask: Do we still enjoy the representation if it is not perfect?

Activity

👤 Show the children **Copymaster 39**. When we look at these pictures we cannot tell whether it is summer or winter. With a little help we could make it clearer.

Ask: What should we draw on the summer scene to make it more realistic? What could we add to the winter scene?

Allow the children to finish the pictures so that they clearly represent the seasons as labelled.

Key teaching point: That to make a representation realistic we have to add careful detail.

Plenary

Share the ideas which the children have put onto each season's image. Make a list.

Ask: Are the finished pictures much more clear? Could they be used now as a background for a computer program?

Session 2   ② ④

Introduction

▦ Suggest to the children that they are going to use a
♣ paint program to make their own computer scene.

52

This could be used as a setting for a game. If it is going to be related to a current topic remind them of the features that this might need.

Ask: *What place do you want to represent on the screen?*

Allow the children to share their ideas.

 Demonstrate briefly how to use the main tools of the paint program.

Activity

Encourage the children to create their own scene, putting as much thought as possible into making it realistic.

Save and print out the finished representations.

Key teaching point: That representations on a computer screen need care to make them as realistic as possible.

Plenary

Display the finished work. Discuss the realistic aspects of the images.

Ask: *What would be too difficult for us to represent?*

It would be hard for us to make the branches move in the wind.

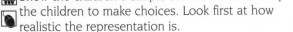

Session 3 ① ③

Introduction

Show the children a simple simulation which requires the children to make choices. Look first at how realistic the representation is.

Ask: *Can we imagine that we are in this place?*

Suggest that even if it is not perfect some care has gone into it and we can enjoy it just the same. Show the children how they will be required to make choices. This may be simply to click on a direction to take a particular route. It may be to pick up items which will be used later in the adventure.

Activity

Give the children **Copymaster 40**. Tell them that they are going to go on an adventure on the computer. When they make a choice they are going to draw what happened in the space provided. Explain that at the end of the lesson they are going to discuss some of their choices, and what happened as a result.

Key teaching point: That the children need to make choices, and that this may affect what happens next.

Plenary

Discuss what they have drawn on their worksheets. Were there any examples of children making different choices at the same point, and therefore getting different results?

Ask: *Would you have done the same thing again if you had a second chance? Do you feel as though you have really been on a little adventure?*

Follow-up activities

• Use the children's representations as a background to a small multimedia presentation.

• Make four scenes which tell a story and build them into a sequence of pages with text under them.

Now you can take the drink.

The *Apple Adventure* is one of two adventures on the *Teacher's Cupboard* Adventure CD-ROM (Sherston). It could be used for both Session 1 and Session 3 in this unit. Here the adventurer has earned a drink to give to a giant.

Adventures and simulations

Year 2

Learning targets

1 ➤➤ to try things out and explore what happens in real and imaginary situations

2 ➤➤ to understand that a computer can be used to represent a wide range of environments and that some are more elaborate than others

3 ➤➤ to understand that a computer model is not an exact replica of the original

Before you start

Subject knowledge

In Unit 20 the children experienced a simple adventure and covered work on producing representations using a computer. They can now use a more complicated adventure, which may contain more choices.

If necessary this unit can be extended by allowing the children to save their adventure, reload it, and continue. If the adventure used is too simple to justify a second visit in Session 2, use another adventure for the second activity.

It may be interesting to plan to use the pictures from Session 3 in Unit 28.

Related Learning Targets units:
KS1 Unit 20 An introduction to modelling

QCA ICT Scheme of work reference:
Builds on Unit 1A An introduction to modelling
Leads to 3D Exploring simulations

Assessment

Were the children willing to try out different choices?
Do the children appreciate the features of a realistic simulation?
Could they use their experience of simulations to help them design their own representation?

Resources

Simulation or adventure program such as the Teacher's Cupboard, The Crown Adventure (Sherston)
Copymaster 41
Copymaster 42

Vocabulary

Simulation, adventure, realistic, choices

Teaching the sessions

Session 1 ①

Introduction

Load the simulation or adventure. Tell the children that they are going to visit a computer generated environment. Load the program and demonstrate how to get started. If they need to *Log In*, show them how to do it. Explain the main features of the simulation, what each icon does, and show them how they will be told what the objective is.

Show them a little of the adventure. If they are going to save and continue the adventure show them how to do this.

Ask: *Is this representation realistic? Can you imagine that you are there, in the environment?*

Activity

Show the children the report that they need to fill out on **Copymaster 41**. Explain that it might be best if they stop and fill it in as they go along. Allow the children to work through the simulation.

Key teaching point: That they can try out decisions and see what happens.

Plenary

Discuss what they wrote down on their report sheets.

Ask: *Where was this adventure set? What choices did you make in the simulation? Did you have to alter any decisions?*

Session 2

Introduction

Remind the children of the previous session. Tell them that they are going to use the same simulation, but make different choices and see what happens.

Ask: *What could you do differently?*

Show them **Copymaster 42** and ask them to keep a record, written or pictorial, of the places they visit, in the order they visited them.

Activity

Using Copymaster 42 as a record, use the adventure for a second time.

Key teaching point: That the representation of the environment has places and objects to make it more realistic.

Plenary

Compare the routes taken by different children.

Ask: *At what point did they make different choices which gave them different routes? How realistic were the representations?*

Session 3

Introduction

Explain that some people's jobs involve creating the adventure/s they have used. These people try to make the adventure as enjoyable and realistic as they can. There are lots of things which affect what they do, but they are always thinking about their audience for the finished program.

Remind the children of work done using a paint package. Explain that they are going to create an environment for an adventure. Decide on a location, for example the seaside. Ask the children to select a specific place to create a background. If using the seaside as the theme, some children might create the funfair, others the beach, others the café and others the caravan park. Ask them to think carefully about what they include.

Activity

Work on the backgrounds, saving them using names which help to identify which background they have created.

Key teaching point: That the environments created should be as realistic as possible.

Plenary

Look at the pictures. Move a *Clip art* picture round on the background to see if it looks realistic.

Ask: *Would the scale be sensible? What did the simulation they used include that their pictures do not?*

Suggest that sound and movement are features which help to bring a simulation alive.

Follow-up activities

* Look at panoramic webcam pictures on the Internet.

* Devise a report sheet of things they could look for in simulations to evaluate them.

Learning targets

1 ➤➤ to know about the uses of ICT inside and outside of school

2 ➤➤ to recognise that some machines and devices work by using a sequence of physical actions

3 ➤➤ to know that instructions can be recorded for amendment and replication

Before you start

QCA ICT Scheme of work reference:
Links to Unit 1F An introduction to modelling

Subject knowledge

This unit formalises the need for children to be aware that technology has an effect on everybody's lives. You will need some relevant items around the classroom ready for Session 1, such as a tape recorder, a CD player, a TV and a video recorder.

If the children are older it may be better to use a more sophisticated device for them to control, rather than the cassette recorder suggested. They could complete an activity using a video recorder, using either the buttons on the recorder or the remote control.

Related Learning Targets units:
This unit is the first in its series. It links with:
KS1 Unit 20 An introduction to modelling

Assessment

Can the children name some devices which use modern technology?
Are the children aware of the need to sequence instructions correctly?
Did the children put the cassette recorder actions into the correct order?

Resources

Cassette recorder and other technological devices
Copymaster 43
Copymaster 44

Vocabulary

Control, technology, devices, correct order

Teaching the sessions

Session 1 ① ②

Introduction

 Look around the classroom for technology which helps us in our everyday lives. Discuss who knows how to work the items that the children spot. It may help to look in the imaginative play area. Are there any more things which help us that they can name? They may refer to cars, washing machines, telephones.

Explain that when working these machines the actions need to be carried out in the right order.

Ask: *Do you know how to use a cassette recorder?*

Ask a child to demonstrate how to play a tape. Include putting the tape in as the first task.

Activity

Look at **Copymaster 43**. These are possible instructions for making a tape recorder work.

Ask: *Can you work out what is happening in each one?*

The instructions are in the wrong order. Try to carry them out as they are.

Ask: *Did they work?*

Ask the children to cut out the pictures and stick them in the correct order.

Key teaching point: That instructions need to be carried out in the correct order to work properly.

Plenary

Check the children's cassette recorder instructions. Ask a child to carry out the instructions as you read them out.

Ask: *Are they all the same? Did you all adjust the volume at the same point?*

Session 2 ① ② ③

Introduction

 Look at **Copymaster 44**. Discuss how technology helps in the illustrated instances.

Ask: *Could these jobs be done just as well by people? What would the disadvantages be?*

Explain how a person could not go round and turn all the street lights on. People could turn the central heating on but it might get too hot or too cold and they would need to keep altering it. See if they can suggest other examples where things happen without anybody seeming to control them.

Ask: *Who makes the lifts in shops go up and down?*

Activity

Ask the children to draw a person next to the things which could easily be controlled by people without machines. Ask them to use a separate piece of paper to draw the machines that they can control. This could include the cassette recorder from the previous session.

Key teaching point: That some machines can work on their own if a series of instructions is recorded for them to follow.

Plenary

Ask the children about their suggestions for things which they can control. Do all of the children agree with them?

Follow-up activities

• Link this to work using a floor robot.

• Make a set of instructions for crossing the road using a pedestrian crossing.

• Use a piece of simulation software which allows them to control a machine.

CD-ROM AND INTERNET

Units 23–28

There is a vast amount of material available for teaching purposes on the internet and on CD-ROMs. However, much of it is totally unsuitable for Key Stage 1 pupils. Even material which is claimed to be suitable is often too hard for the children to read and far too hard for them to navigate. However, if resources are carefully produced there is no reason why the ICT aspect of finding information from CD-ROMs and the Internet cannot be carried out satisfactorily.

For this reason it is important to examine resources before buying them. Find places where the presentation and content of CD-ROMs in particular can be tried out. Read reviews. Once suitable CD-ROMs have been located, if cost is a problem, remember that a small number of quality resources is better than a larger amount that cannot really be used.

Resource Issues

When using websites find and bookmark the sites that give pupils a chance to practise using hyperlinks, whilst at the same time benefiting from the material contained on the website. If you cannot locate sites suited to the children's needs then you should seriously consider making your own material. Pupils love the advantages of being able to navigate the pages in their own order, rather than a prescribed order. A few web pages suitably hyperlinked can benefit children much more than many pages which are like a maze to them. Use educational sources to help locate sites. *Learning Alive's Pathways* and the MAPE website (***www.mape.org.uk***) are particularly useful.

As you will know, you cannot always guarantee internet access in schools, and there are still times when schools with well developed computer systems find that their Internet Service Provider (ISP) is temporarily not functioning. There is also the possibility of unsuitable material appearing on the computer screens. These are all good reasons for either saving sites to the computer's hard drive, or constructing your own websites which can also be stored on the computer's hard drive. Although this can be daunting at first there are plenty of help menus and articles to help with setting this up.

Teaching Issues

Younger children can often be put off when they have typed a URL in several times and failed to connect to the site they are meant to be looking at. You can take the tedium out of this process by adding the URL to Favourites, ready for the children to use. This also ensures that good sites are not forgotten, and continue to be used.

The problem of unsuitable material reaching the children continues to be a hazard. Using a filtered ISP, but hopefully one that will not inhibit learning too much, is essential. However it is still very important when going onto the World Wide Web with children to check the URLs to be used as close to the lesson as possible. Websites now have an unpleasant habit of being taken over and replaced with suspect material in order to access previous users of the site. This problem cannot be emphasised enough.

Cross-curricular Links

English

Fiction reading can be developed using ICT resources. These can give help with reading and provide an interesting stimulus with the inclusion of multimedia.

- Talking books give opportunities to listen to stories, read stories and explore the surroundings.
- Big Books for use in the literacy hour are available. Many of these can be found on web sites such as the MAPE website. These allow pupils to see the books clearly during the shared reading sessions.

Science

CD-ROMs and the Internet can be used to provide excellent information sources. They also can be used as a source of activities to develop specific scientific skills.
- There are some excellent CD-ROMs developed with Key Stage 1 children in mind, and that can support the Science curriculum. In particular *All about Ourselves* and *All about the Weather and Seasons* (both SEMERC) are excellent for science work and ICT skills development.

History

As in science work there are both sources of information and interactive activities which support the history curriculum.
- Look at websites which show the seaside through the last hundred years.
- Researching significant people for studying at Key Stage 1 is much easier when using web-sites. This information could then easily be made into a multimedia presentation.

Art

The World Wide Web makes access to art all over the world possible. It also gives access to resources, such as related colouring pictures.
- Use the World Wide Web to visit art galleries round the world. Particularly useful are the virtual tours where viewers even see pictures hanging on the walls and can move from room to room. Some of these sites are also available on CD-ROM.
- Find out about the lives of artists.

Music

The ability to include sounds both on websites and CD-ROMs makes them suitable for use in music lessons. The World Wide Web gives access to museums which relate to famous composers.
- Research the different ways in which sound is produced, looking at instruments which are blown, plucked or banged etc.
- Find out about a famous composer.

RE

You can access a range of resources for teaching about different religions. These often include resource sheets for use with the children.
- Find pictures of the different buildings which relate to various religions.
- Look at the artefacts which relate to particular religions.
- See how different people round the world celebrate festivals. Is Christmas the same in the UK and America?

PSHE

Many charities which are concerned with this have excellent interactive websites. They also publish material on CD-ROM.
- Research the aspects of road safety and keeping safe in the home.
- Find out about healthy eating.
- See what charities are doing to help sections of society and those in need round the world.

Recognising information

Reception

Learning targets

1 ➤➤ to use information technology to support their learning

2 ➤➤ to recognise that information can be presented in a variety of forms

3 ➤➤ to understand that information comes from a variety of sources

Before you start

Subject knowledge

As a very early introduction to finding information from a computer this work is kept very simple. The children may not have had much experience of computers at all. Introduce the general idea that a computer can be controlled through the keyboard and the mouse, and that information is shown on the screen.

Select CD-ROMs which achieve learning objectives, whilst at the same time being fun for younger children to use. CD-ROMs that use sounds will motivate and interest children; however the noise from activities such as these can be very overpowering. Using headphones can be helpful, if necessary with an adapter to allow two children to listen to the same sounds together.

Related Learning Targets units:
This unit is the first in its series. It leads to:
KS1 Unit 24 *Using a CD-ROM*

QCA ICT Scheme of work reference:
Links to Unit 1C *The information around us*

Assessment

Can the children use hotspots to navigate a CD-ROM?
Are the children able to guess where a sound might be in a talking book?
Do the children understand the difference between a book and an information CD-ROM?

Resources

Information CD-ROM such as *My First Incredible Amazing Dictionary* (DK)
Talking book such as *Just Grandma and Me* (Broderbund)
Copymaster 45
Copymaster 46

Vocabulary

CD-ROM, sounds, hotspot, hyperlink, headphones

Teaching the sessions

Session 1

Introduction

Look at a simple picture book containing information. Discuss how it tells us about a particular subject. Look at the pictures and the text. Turn the pages.

Ask: *Can we can find out about things from books?*

Use a very simple CD-ROM containing information. Demonstrate the ways in which the icons and hyperlinks can be used to get to different pages. This will vary from program to program. Explain how some of the icons are pictures to give us clues as to what they lead to. Show the children how to use the *home*

icon, if there is one, to get back to the first page if they get 'lost'.

Activity

Use **Copymaster 45**. Ask the children to use the CD-ROM to find out something interesting. They may discover something they did not know. Ask them to write, copy or draw something which they found useful.

Key teaching point: That information can be presented in a variety of forms.

Plenary

Ask the children if having the sounds made the activity more interesting.

Ask: *Which sounds were best? Did they help to explain part of the story?*

Session 2

Introduction

 Look at a simple storybook, turning the pages and reading the text or telling the story. Comment on any points where sounds are mentioned or could be used.

Ask: *Wouldn't it be nice to hear the sounds?*

Demonstrate a talking book. Go through the first few pages of the story. Comment on the way the text is read for the user. Ask the children if they enjoy listening to the sounds.

Activity

Allow the children to use the talking book. Let them turn the pages and listen to the story. If the facility is available let them 'explore' the page, and encourage them to listen to the sounds.

Key teaching point: That computers can use various types of media.

Plenary

Look at another picture book. Ask the children for ideas about how it could be turned into a talking book. How would this improve the book?

Session 3

Introduction

 Look at **Copymaster 46**. It shows a busy street scene.

Ask: *What sounds might they be hearing if they were really in the street?*

Ask if they think that the computer could add sounds to these.

Activity

Ask the children to colour in the objects in the street scene on Copymaster 46 which would make a noise in real life.

Key teaching point: That sound makes images more realistic.

Plenary

Look at a large poster of a scene. Ask the children to suggest sounds for this picture.

Follow-up activities
- Investigate musical instruments to see what they sound like.
- Prepare a picture for the children to use with sound effects activated by hotspots.

Using a CD-ROM

Year 1

Learning targets

1 ➤➤ to be able to gather information from a variety of sources
2 ➤➤ to recognise that CD-ROMs hold large amounts of information
3 ➤➤ to be able to use an index or key words to locate information

Before you start

Subject knowledge

This builds on the introduction in Unit 23. Here the children use the index of the CD-ROM to locate information. The emphasis is on the speed at which the CD-ROM can locate the information and the way in which the key word has to be selected carefully.

Whenever possible select CD-ROMs which are intended for Key Stage 1. Using encyclopaedias such as *Encarta* causes frustration. If these adult reference tools do have to be used, direct the pupils to search for items which you have checked will bring up a picture relevant to their topic.

You may wish to prepare Copymaster 47 with some words which you know are in the A–Z of the CD-ROM being used.

Related Learning Targets units:
KS1 Unit 23 *Recognising information*
KS1 Unit 25 *Features of CD-ROMs*
QCA ICT Scheme of work reference:
Leads to Unit 2C *Finding information*

Assessment

Can the children suggest sensible key words to search for?
Did the children appreciate the various types of media used to get over the information?

Resources

Reference CD-ROMs
Copymaster 47
Copymaster 48

Vocabulary

CD-ROM, sound, animation, video, index, links

Teaching the sessions

Session 1

Introduction

▨ Briefly look at an information book with an index.
◐ Show how key words relating to the topic covered in the book are all listed in the index. Show how the list gives the pages where these topics can be found. Load the reference CD-ROM that the children are going to use.

Ask: *How do you think we could use an A–Z index on the computer.*

◥ Demonstrate how to use the A–Z search facility. Show how it takes you to the relevant information.

Activity

▨▨ Show the children **Copymaster 47**. Ask them to use ◐ the CD-ROM to find out something for each letter. Remind them of the topic that they are researching. Give them ideas of useful things to try to find out. Explain that they would not want to look for ordinary words such as 'the' or 'which'. They want to search for words linked to the topic. Ask them to copy some of the information they found onto the worksheet. This may be in the form of a sentence or a picture.

Help the children as they use the CD-ROM and enter the words they searched for onto the worksheet.

Key teaching point: That using an index on a CD-ROM finds information quickly.

Plenary

Compare the finished worksheets.

Ask: *Did everybody find out something? Were there any useful topic words not found in the index?*

Session 2

Introduction

▨ In this session the children will use the techniques ⚅ learnt in Session 1 to find out useful information for a topic. They will use the index to answer questions set by you. Remind them that they will need to think of a useful word to search for. This word must have something to do with the questions being asked. You may wish to give different groups different questions to research.

Ask: *How did we use the A–Z index?*

Remind them of how to use the index.

Activity

Set the children working on the questions. Ask them to check with the teacher before printing out the information, which can be used for a display or topic information book. Remind them how to print out from the CD-ROM.

Key teaching point: That only a carefully chosen word will produce results when searching for information.

Plenary

Share the printouts with the whole group.

Ask: *Did they find out some useful information?*

Session 3 ❶ ❷

Introduction

Look at the same CD-ROM. Investigate the different ways of locating information on a topic. For these they may need to know a little more about the topic. They may need to know whether they are researching a geography or a history topic. For example, they may need to know that the animal they are researching is a bird. Work together on finding

sections on two or three areas of their topic. Look at the links to the information.

Remind the children that one advantage of using a computer based information source is that they may also find sounds, images, animations and videos. Another is that it can hold lots of information. It can contain as much information a whole set of books.

Locate one or two.

Activity

Ask the children to choose their own way of locating information on their topic. Ask them to record a selection of things they found onto **Copymaster 48**. Encourage them to make sure that this includes one sound.

Key teaching point: That CD-ROMs contain lots of information in a variety of formats.

Plenary

Discuss what was found.

Ask: *What was the most unusual thing you found out? Which sounds did you find? Did anybody find any animations or videos?*

Follow-up activities
• Repeat the activities above using different CD-ROMs.
• Make an A–Z of information on a topic using information from a CD-ROM.

Features of CD-ROMS

Year 2

Learning targets

1 ➡ to be able to retrieve information that has been stored

2 ➡ to be able to use an index or key words to locate information

3 ➡ to use hyperlinks to navigate a CD-ROM

4 ➡ to understand that information can be connected in different ways at the same time

Before you start

Subject knowledge

This work builds on previous work on using CD-ROMs. It will be necessary to reinforce what has gone before, as these information skills are not easy.

On some CD-ROMs the A–Z index is replaced by another searchable list. This can vary greatly, depending on what CD-ROM is being used. For example, if using the *Kingfisher Micropedia* (ESM Software) the list of subjects would be used as an alternative.

Related Learning Targets units:
KS1 Unit 24 *Using a CD-ROM*
QCA ICT Scheme of work reference:
Unit 2C *Finding information*

Assessment

Are the children able to use the A–Z index?
Can the children find information by using the hyperlinks on a CD-ROM?
Did the children appreciate the different types of media on a CD-ROM?

Resources

Information CD-ROMs
Atlas CD-ROM
Copymaster 49
Copymaster 50

Vocabulary

A–Z index, icons, Home Page, hotspots, hyperlinks

Teaching the sessions

Session 1

Introduction

▦ Load the CD-ROM that the children are going to be using.

Ask: *How can I find out about our topic using this CD-ROM?*

Explain that the CD-ROM is organised a bit like a book. It has an index to take us to where particular words can be found. It also has a way of taking us to sections of the CD-ROM which might be helpful to us.

Show the children how to work through the menus, using either icons or hyperlinked text. Demonstrate the quick method of getting back to the Home Page. This is usually by use of an icon. Show how to use the back button to go to the previous pages.

Activity

Allow the children time to explore the CD-ROM.

Either direct them to a topic or let them investigate subjects of interest to them. Stop them periodically and ask them to think about how they got to the page they are on.

Key teaching point: That there are various routes to finding information on a CD-ROM.

Plenary

Ask the children if they can describe something interesting which they found. Can they also describe how the rest of the children could get to that information if they wanted to?

Ask: *Which method did you use most? Were the links to various sections useful and understandable?*

Session 2

Introduction

▦ In this session the children will use a hyperlinked map to find information about a place. Load a digital atlas such as the *Dorling Kindersley World Reference Atlas*. Show the children how to identify a country using either the A–Z index or the hyperlinked map of the world.

Ask: *When might you want to use the hyperlinked map?*

Explain that if you know a country's name, but not where it is, you would want to use the A–Z index. If you knew the shape of a country and where it was on the map, you might want to click on the map to find out what the country was.

Activity

Give the children **Copymaster 49**. Tell them that they are going to use the computer to help them to find the names of some countries, and then find where some other countries are. They will be able to fill in the boxes on the map with the countries' names. They will be able to label the two countries written on the worksheet.

Demonstrate how you would find India if you were asked to label it. Use the A–Z index.

Demonstrate how if you wanted to know the name of a country on a map you could use the *hotspots* on the map.

Key teaching point: That there may be more than one route to information on a CD-ROM.

Plenary

Have all the children got the same answers on the Copymaster? If any are wrong, investigate to see if they were very close.

Session 3

Introduction

Select a CD-ROM which has various types of media. If possible make it one which has the facility to search for particular media types. Tell the children that this time they are only going to search for video clips. Explain what these are.

Activity

Demonstrate how to search for video clips. Explain how to play them and how to shut them down.

Ask the children to search for and to record on **Copymaster 50** the video clips they find. They can record them either as text or with a picture of the subject of the video.

Key teaching point: That CD-ROMs can enable the user to locate examples of a particular type of media.

Plenary

Have the computer ready loaded with the CD-ROM. Ask the children what they found. Locate it and play it on the computer for the other children to see.

Ask: *Why might we want to find video clips? What other types of media might we want to locate?*

Follow-up activities

• Use various CD-ROMs, experimenting with their different layouts and icons.

• Look in catalogues to see what other information CD-ROMs are available.

• Research a topic.

An introduction to the Internet

Year 1

Learning targets

1 ➤➤ to be able to gather information from a variety of sources

2 ➤➤ to recognise that computers use text, pictures and sounds to convey information

Before you start

Subject knowledge

Young children enjoy seeing things they recognise on the computer. Looking at the school website or a local authority Tourist Information website will be fun for them. See more details on ways of making this activity more practical in the Introduction. If necessary navigate the website for them, sitting them so that they can clearly see the screen.

Looking more closely at the style of the website helps the children to realise that it can be made up of several pages. They will recognise this by noting the similarity of style on the pages.

Related Learning Targets units:
This unit is the first in its series. It links to:
KS1 Unit 24 *Using a CD-ROM*
KS1 Unit 27 *Using the Internet*

QCA ICT Scheme of work reference:
Unit 1C *The information around us*

Assessment

Were the children able to navigate the website using the buttons and other links?
Did the children appreciate that websites can convey up-to-date information?

Resources

Information CD-ROM
Internet browser and Internet access
Suitable URLs
Copymaster 51
Copymaster 52

Vocabulary

Website, web page, Home Page, button, hyperlink

Teaching the sessions

Session 1 ①

Introduction

Look at a CD-ROM that the children have used. Have a look at how old the CD-ROM is. Explain that this information may be out of date now. New things may not be on it. It is hard to add things to a CD-ROM. Explain that if we want to see really up-to-date things we can look on the World Wide Web. Look, if possible, at the school website. Otherwise look at a local authority website with pictures of the local area.

Ask: *Who produces this? How easy is it to change it?*

Explain that ordinary people can make a website and include pictures of their favourite things on it. Information can also be put on the website, such as the train times or what is on at the cinema.

Activity

Demonstrate how to navigate a website. Explain that they can click on the buttons to go to new pages. Show them how to get back to the *Home Page*.

Ask the children to explore the site. Give them **Copymaster 51**. Ask them to draw something which they saw on the website that they have also seen in real life. This may be the school building or a local landmark.

Key teaching point: That websites can be, but are not always, very up-to-date.

Plenary

Show the children another similar local website which will be of interest to them. Discuss what is shown on the pages. Show them how the buttons on this website work.

Session 2 ①②

Introduction

Locate suitable websites on a topic being covered by the children. If necessary use Local Educational Authority's websites or Education Internet Service Providers' websites to help locate suitable sites. Choose them for their interesting features, especially chosen to please children. An excellent site is the website of Snaith Primary School (***www.snaithprimary.eril.net***).

Explain to the children that they may be able to click on pictures, words or buttons. Usually a hand appears to show them that they can click on something. Explain that this is called a hyperlink.

Move the cursor over the screen to demonstrate.

Explain that when people build a website they choose what sort of buttons they want, and what colour background and writing they think suits their website.

Activity

Allow the children to explore the website that they are allocated to. Ask them to fill in **Copymaster 52** to record details about the style of the website. This includes the background colour, writing colour, button style and one picture seen.

Key teaching point: That websites are constructed to suit the topic they cover.

Plenary

Report back on what the website they looked at was like.

Ask: *Had anybody got very unusual buttons on their website? Were any of the backgrounds special?*

Discuss whether these were chosen because of what the website was about. For example, were frogs chosen because the website was about the adventures a frog exploring a river?

Follow-up activities

- Repeat the activities above using different websites.
- Design a paper version of a Home Page for their own website.
- Print out and label the features of some of the more unusual websites that the children have investigated.

Using the Internet

Year 2

Learning targets

1 ➤➤ to be able to gather information from a variety of sources

2 ➤➤ to be aware of search techniques to find information

3 ➤➤ to be aware that websites can present information in different ways

Before you start

Subject knowledge

This unit reinforces the skills learnt in Unit 26. It gives more practice and also includes an extension activity for children ready to learn about searching the Internet.

Before the lesson find two contrasting locality websites. If possible bookmark them so that children can simply go to *Favourites* and click on them. Fill in the two place names and URLs on the Copymaster 53 before photocopying it.

For Session 3 carry out a search beforehand. Have a few key words in mind that the children may suggest relating to the current term's topics. Make a note of what websites come up. Investigate them and find the best ones to show to the children. Carry out the search near to the time of the lesson. See if some of the same sites come up, and make a note to use them.

Related Learning Targets units:
KS1 Unit 26 *An introduction to the Internet*
KS2 Unit 4 *Writing to inform*
QCA ICT Scheme of work reference:
Links to Unit 2C *Finding information*

Assessment

Can the children locate information from websites? Did the children appreciate the need for a search engine to locate suitable websites?

Resources

Two contrasting locality websites
Web browser and internet access
Copymaster 53
Copymaster 54

Vocabulary

Website, button, background, search engine

Teaching the sessions

Session 1 ①

Introduction

Remind the children of the ways that a website can be navigated. Demonstrate using buttons, hyperlinked text and hyperlinked pictures. Remind them that the hand will appear when there is something that can be clicked on.

Tell them that they are going to find out about a place. They are going to look at two websites and find out what sort of transport is there. They will be able to look at pictures and read some writing.

Show the children how to access *Favourites* and how to click on the site they need.

Activity

 Show the children **Copymaster 53**. Ask them to investigate the two places by looking at the pages of the website. Remind them that the colours and buttons should stay the same unless they accidentally go off the website. They should use the back button if this happens. Ask them to draw the vehicles found in the two places on Copymaster 53.

Key teaching point: That information can be found on the World Wide Web.

Plenary

Bring the class together to discuss their findings. Use a display board to record all the evidence of forms of transport.

Ask: *Was there a type of transport which both places had?*
Was there a type that one place had but not the other?

Point out that the absence of information on a website does not necessarily mean that that information does not exist.

Session 2

Introduction

Look at the design of a topical website. Notice how the background, buttons, and decorative features fit in with the topic. Look at another good example of unusual web design.

Activity

 Show the children **Copymaster 54**. Tell the children that they are going to design their own website on paper. Show the spaces for them to draw their own special sort of buttons.

Let the children decide on a name for their website first. Tell them it can be about a hobby, a topic, a place or a person. When they design it they will have to take their choice of subject into consideration.

Ask: *What colour will you do your background? What will your pages be called?*

Key teaching point: That website design depends on the subject matter and the likes and dislikes of the webmaster.

Plenary

Look at the various designs. Which ones fit their topic well?

Ask: *Which ones would be fun to visit?*

Tell the children that some websites have buttons which move when you click on them. Some even make sounds.

Session 3

Introduction

 Ask the children how they think you found the websites they have been using in their lessons. There are far too many websites for them all to be in a book like the telephone directory. There are some lists of websites, but there would be lots of sites not on the lists.

Activity

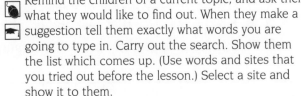 Show the children how a search engine works. Remind the children of a current topic, and ask them what they would like to find out. When they make a suggestion tell them exactly what words you are going to type in. Carry out the search. Show them the list which comes up. (Use words and sites that you tried out before the lesson.) Select a site and show it to them.

Key teaching point: That search engines help to locate useful websites.

Plenary

Point out that when people find a useful website they add it to their *Favourites* so that they can use it again.

Follow-up activities

- Use a paint program to design the main features of a website.
- Arrange to have some of the children's work put onto the school website so that they can see their own work there.

Simple multimedia

Year 2

Learning targets

1 ➡➡ to be able to review and modify what they have done to help them develop ideas

2 ➡➡ to understand that text and graphics can be combined to communicate information

3 ➡➡ to be able to combine text and graphics

Before you start

Subject knowledge

This activity will be greatly enhanced with a little extra planning and careful structuring. There are many software packages which could be used. These range from the software already used for word processing, such as *Textease* 2000, to software specifically designed for multimedia presentations. If using a program such as *PowerPoint* (Microsoft) it would be best if the basic pages were first prepared and saved by you. The children could then simply add the subject matter.

Related Learning Targets units:
This unit is the first in its series. It links to:
KS1 Unit 3 *Word processing skills*
KS2 Unit 9 *Story starts*

QCA ICT Scheme of work reference:
Leads to Unit 3A *Combining text and graphics*

Assessment

Could the children suggest material suitable for their presentations?
Were the comments made about each other's presentations helpful and constructive?

Resources

Multimedia Program
Multimedia resources; *Clip art*, photographs, sounds, animations, videos
Copymaster 55
Copymaster 56

Vocabulary

Presentation, background, links, hyperlink, multimedia

Teaching the sessions

Session 1 ② ③

Introduction

Show the children an example of a multimedia program. Point out the various types of media. These may include text, sounds, video, images, and animations. Explain the term *multimedia*.

Demonstrate how a contents page leads to the other pages. Show how a link on the other pages leads back to the contents page.

Can you think of a topic which you could use to make a multimedia presentation?

Activity

Show the children **Copymaster 55**. Explain that they can plan a simple presentation using this worksheet. Tell them that they will need a title for their presentation, and a title for each of the two pages of information. They will need to think of something to put onto the pages. This can be pictures, text or any other media available. They can decide on a colour

for their background, and a colour for their writing. They should fill in the names of the two pages on the Contents page.

The children work in pairs to design their presentation.

Key teaching point: That designing a presentation needs planning and can include a variety of media.

Plenary

Look at the various designs. Have they filled in the areas they need to? Are the two pages on a similar subject?

Session 2 ① ③

Introduction

Before the lesson check the children's plans, and make adjustments where necessary. Show the children the prepared presentation. Show them how the links already work. Indicate the items that they will need to change. Give them their plans from Session 1 and ask them which things are different. Tell them that they will be able to change those easily.

Ask: *How can you change the background colour?*

Demonstrate how to change the background colour and the colour of the text.

Activity

Direct the children to save the presentation using a name which fits their topic. Talk them through this step by step.

Encourage the children to use their plan to modify the presentation and make it their own.

Key teaching point: That text and graphics can be combined.

Plenary

Look at a few of the children's finished presentations alongside their plans. Judge how they match up and ask why any changes were made.

Session 3

Introduction

Before the lesson make a list of all of the presentations. Make them available to all the children.

Tell the children that they are going to look at each other's presentations. They are going to see if the work fits the task they were set.

Demonstrate how to load the presentations.

Activity

Show the children **Copymaster 56**. Explain that they are going to look at some of the presentations and tick the boxes, or colour them in to show what colour was used. Read the text.

The children load and review the presentations. They try out the links and see what each page shows.

Key teaching point: That by looking at their work they may see what they did well and what could be improved.

Plenary

Ask the children which presentations were their favourites.

Ask: *What made you pick those ones in particular? Did you fill in all the details on your review sheets?*

Follow-up activities

* Make pages of information with text and pictures that the teacher can link into a presentation.

* Look at some presentations from other sources.

Cut out and use the labels.

table	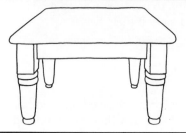
chair	
door	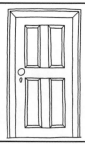
window	
book	
teddy	

72

2 Typing

Type the words. Type your name.

cat

C A T

dog

D O G

cup

C U P

sun

S U N

car

C A R

home

H O M E

Type your name –

play	run	children	skip

playground	ball	throw	catch

The Windy Day

I walk up the street,
I wobble on my feet,
The trees bend low
As on my way I go.

Leaves whiz by,
Clouds fly across the sky,
Washing flies away
On this very windy day.

by Angella Streluk

Type a snowman story.

snowman, children, scarf, hat,
finished, sun, melt, sad

77

Choose colours to colour the picture.
Try not to go over the lines.

Drawing a picture on the computer.

You can use the shapes tool on the computer to make a shape pattern.

We can use the fill and spray tools.

81

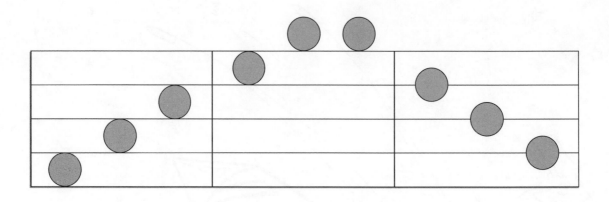

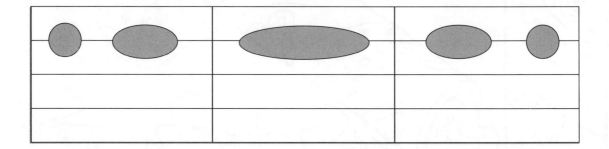

Notes can be higher or lower.
Notes can be longer or shorter.
Make your own tune.

Composing music

Make your own fairground music.
Remember –
think about making it
quiet, loud, fast or slow.
Use long notes and short notes.

83

Write a message to a friend.

This message is to – _____

My message –

This message is from – _____

E-mail addresses

Find some e-mail addresses.

E-mail address	Whose e-mail address is this?

In all of the e-mail addresses I can see a

Draw a line from each animal to its home.

Colour things that can be eaten.

Draw a line to join each object to the correct label.

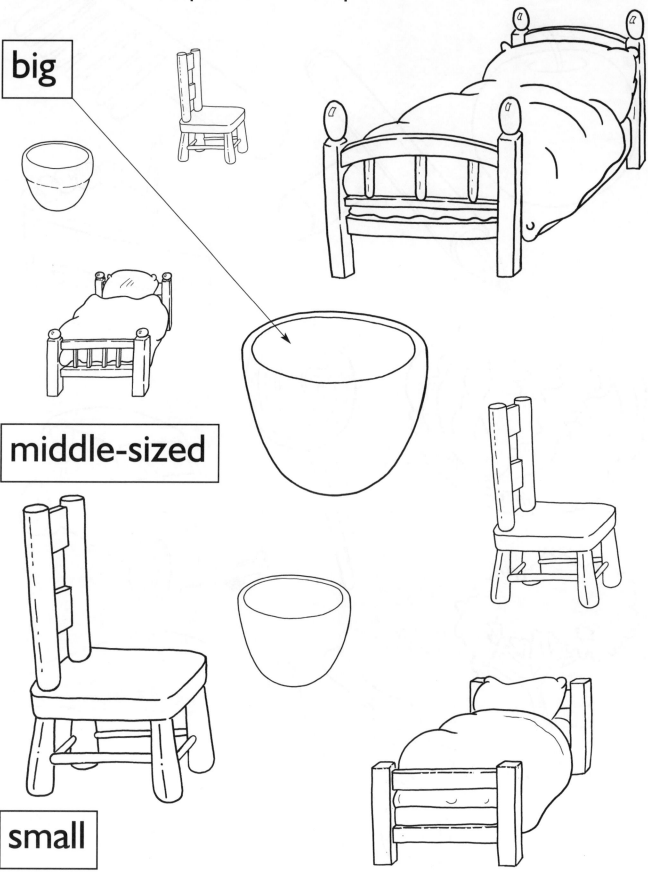

big

middle-sized

small

Draw and colour these shapes.

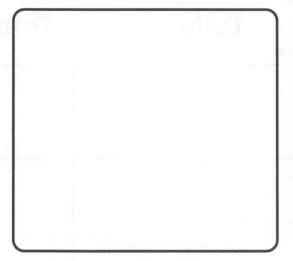

a red circle

a green square

a blue triangle

a yellow oblong

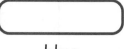

blue

green

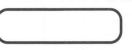

red

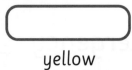

yellow

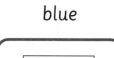

oblong

triangle

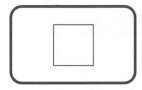

square

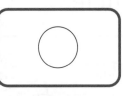

circle

Make a tally of the vehicles you see.

Vehicles	Tally	Total
car		
lorry		
bicycle		
bus		
van		
emergency vehicle		
motor bike		

My survey report

Use your vehicle survey data to write a report.

The vehicle we saw most of was the

_____ .

The vehicle we saw least of was the

_____ .

We saw the same number of —————s

and —————s.

I also noticed that ————————————

————————————————————

bicycle

bus

lorry

motor bike

Place the objects in the correct part of the Venn diagram.

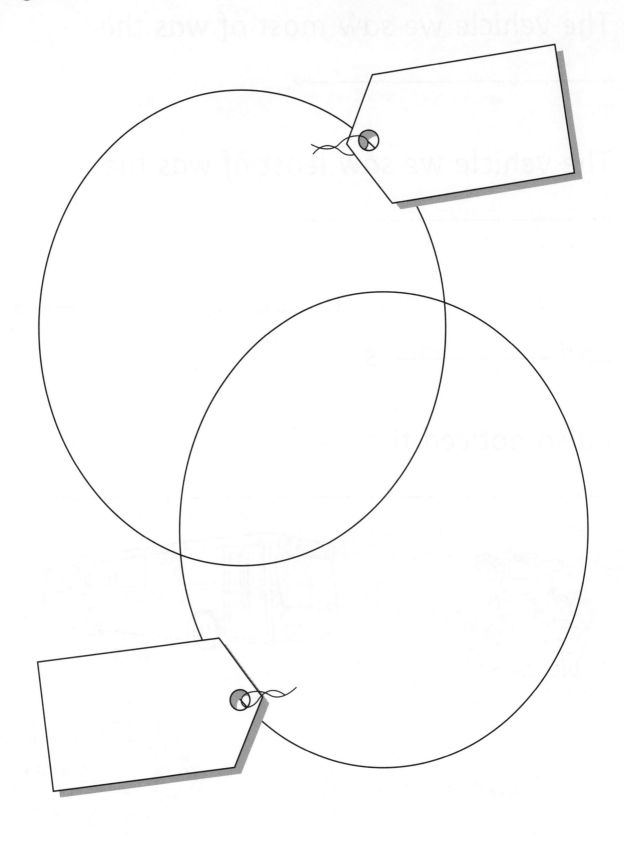

Sorting animals

Sort the animals in two different ways.

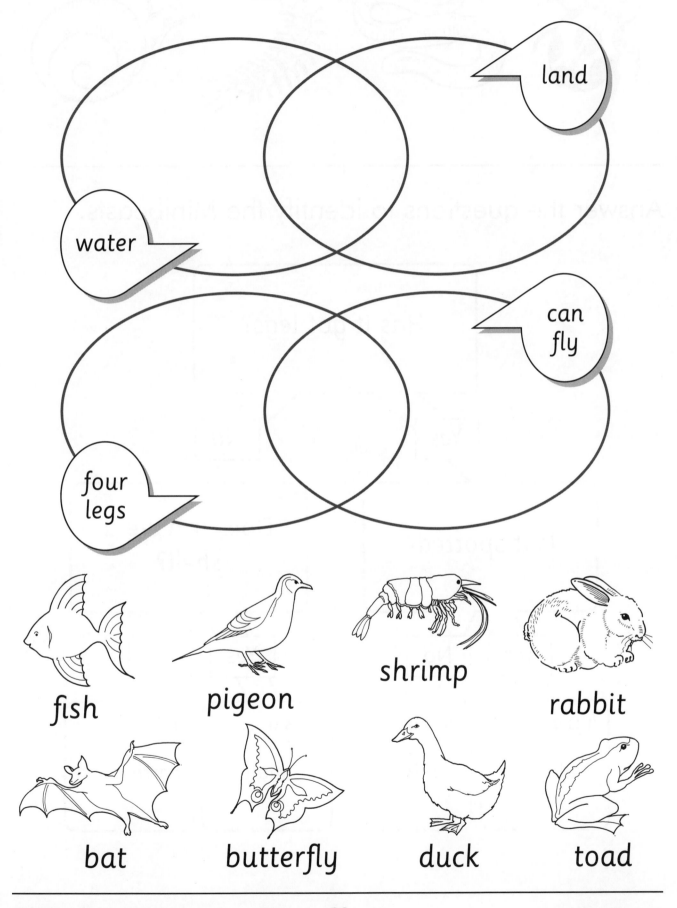

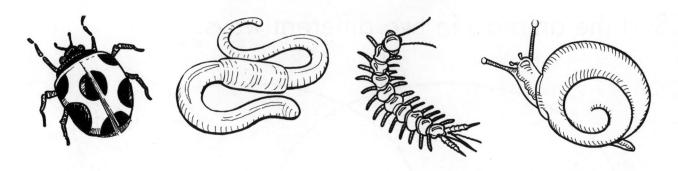

Answer the questions to identify the Minibeasts.

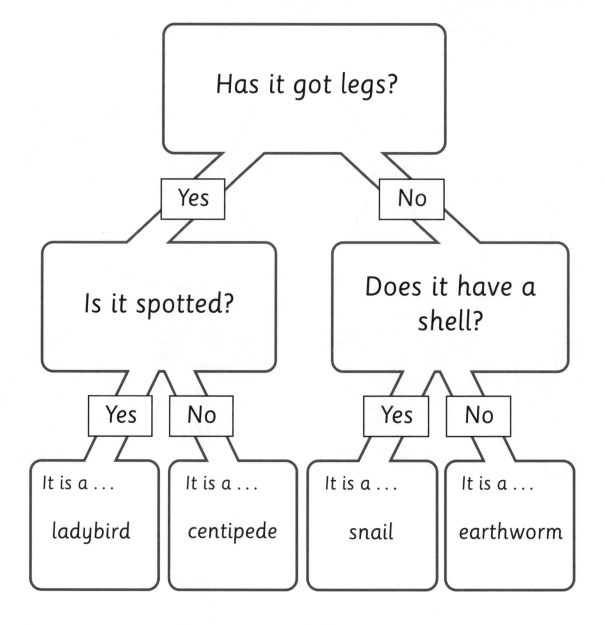

Has it got legs?

Yes

No

Is it spotted?

Does it have a shell?

Yes

No

Yes

No

It is a . . .

ladybird

It is a . . .

centipede

It is a . . .

snail

It is a . . .

earthworm

Binary database

Answer the questions.
Follow the tracks.

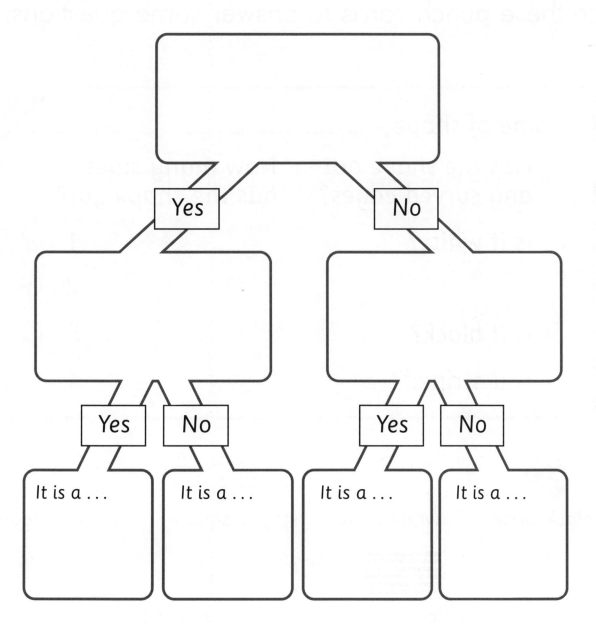

Prepare the punch card for a shape.
Cut out the slot if the answer is 'yes'.
Use these punch cards to answer some questions.

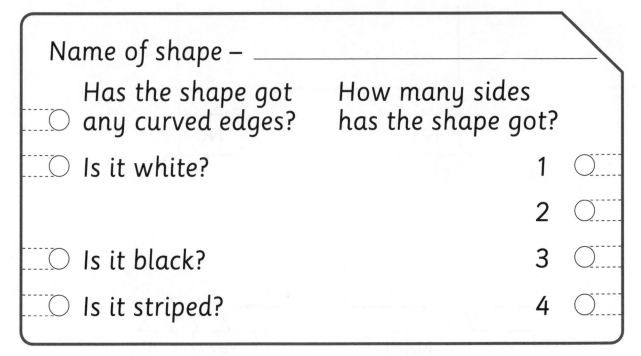

Name of shape – _____

| Has the shape got any curved edges? | How many sides has the shape got? |

○ Has the shape got any curved edges?

○ Is it white?

○ Is it black?

○ Is it striped?

1 ○
2 ○
3 ○
4 ○

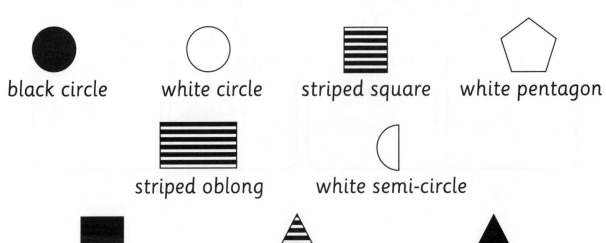

black circle   white circle   striped square   white pentagon

striped oblong   white semi-circle

 black square   striped triangle    black triangle

Punch card database

Add questions to the punch card. Cut out the slot if the answer is 'yes'. Use the punch cards to answer some questions.

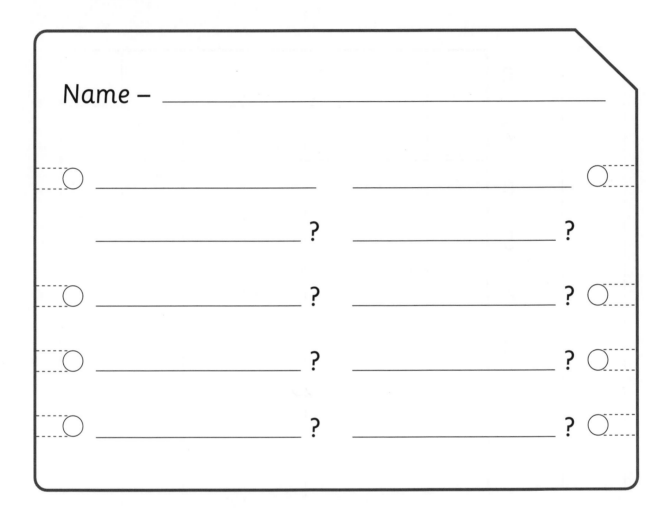

When you sort your punch cards thread them onto your dowelling. Give them a little shake. Those which fall off will have the answer 'yes'.

You can sort these few cards again using another question.

97

Fill in the two labels on the bar chart.
Colour in your data.
Add a title.

8						
7						
6						
5						
4						
3						
2						
1						

Title – _____

Use the circle below to make a pie chart.
Add a title.
Label each section.

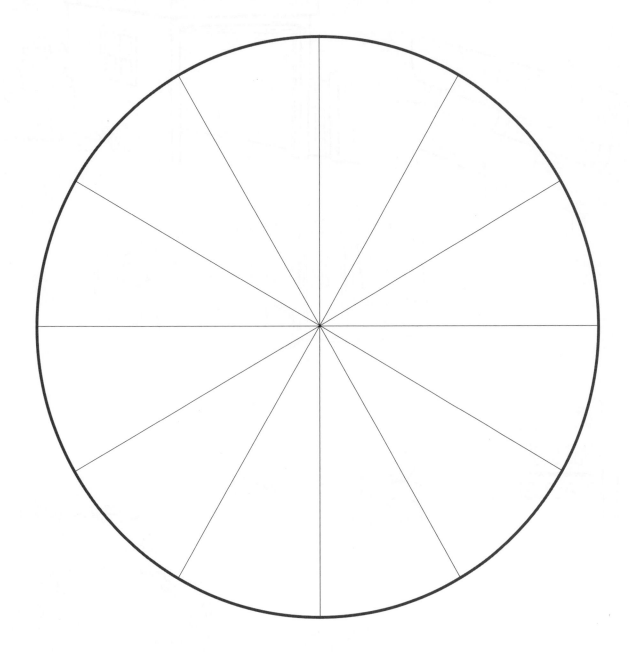

Title –_____

Look at the pictures.
Circle the things that people can control.

Moving Vehicles

Draw lines to take the vehicles to their homes.

Following directions

Use the directions below to help you to direct somebody to a certain place. Cut them out and put them in the right order. Use the blanks for other commands you may need.

Start at _____	Face the _____
Go forward _____ steps	Turn right
Go forward _____ steps	Turn right
Go forward _____ steps	Turn left
Go backwards _____ steps	Turn left
Go backwards _____ steps	You are at _____

Plan a route to take a floor robot from one place to another. Add each command in the correct order.

The robot will start at _____

It will be facing _____

Command 1 –

Command 2 –

Command 3 –

Command 4 –

Command 5 –

Command 6 –

Command 7 –

Command 8 –

Command 9 –

Command 10 –

Commands you might use –

Forward 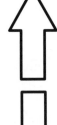   right

Backward 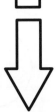   left

Write directions to move a counter from the start to the finish.

✁ -

My instructions –

Cut out your counter

Drawing a shape

Write directions for the floor robot to draw a shape. The shape must start and finish at the X. Follow the lines and count the squares.

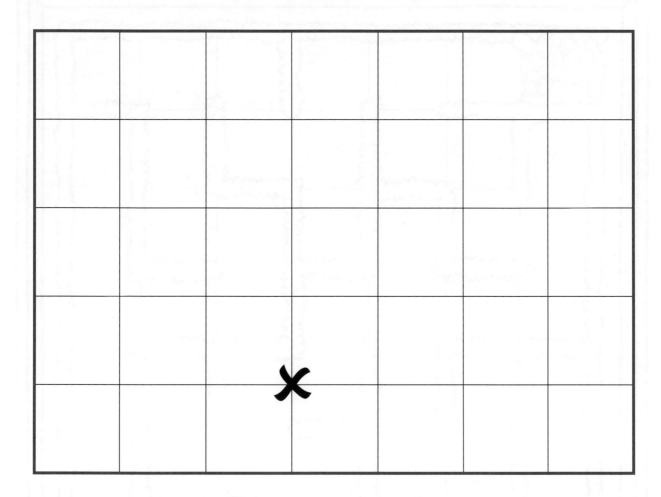

My instructions –

Long or short?

Work out a route. Use the counter. Tell a friend how to move the counter to get to the lettuce.

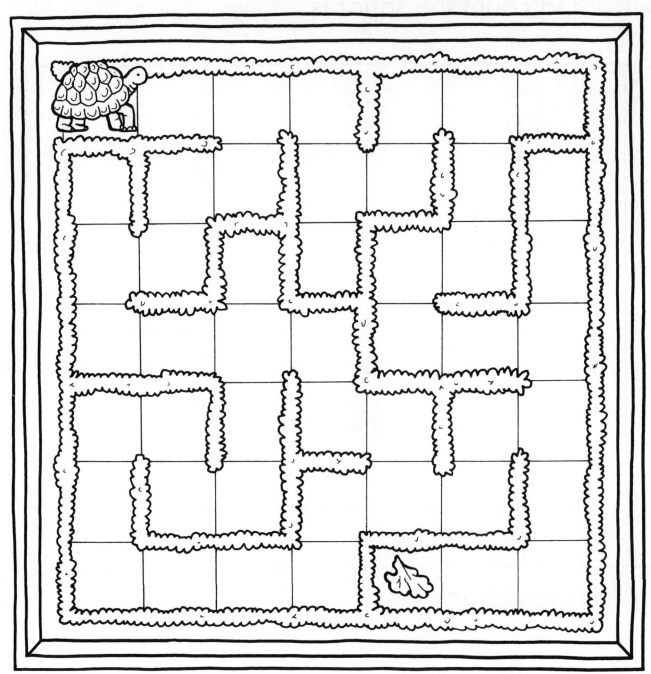

Cut out your counter

Copying shapes

Write directions for the screen turtle so that it can draw these shapes. Start at the X. Count the squares so that you know how far it has to go.

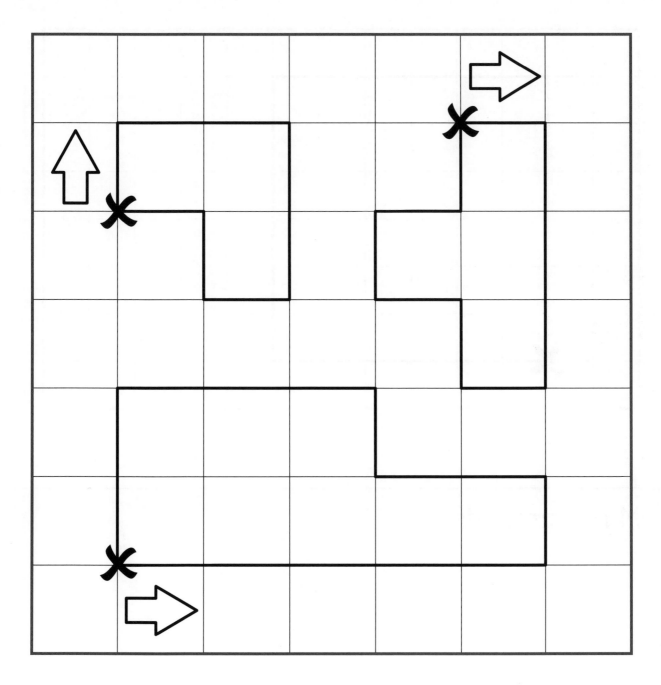

Saving commands

Write directions for the screen turtle so that it can draw this shape. Save the commands so that you can draw the shape again. Start at X.

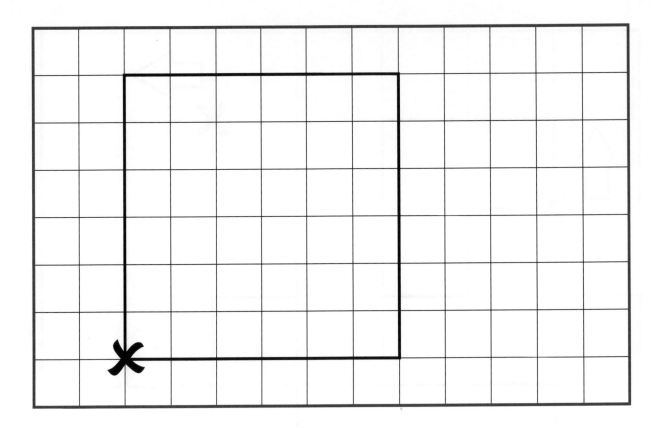

My commands –

108

Plan a shape. Write the directions for the screen turtle so that it can draw the shape. Save your commands.

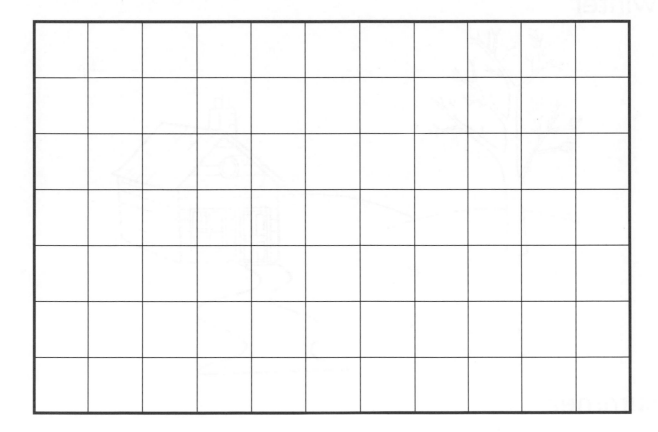

My commands –

Finish the pictures.
Make one look like winter.
Make one look like summer.

winter

summer

What did you choose to do?
Draw two of your choices.
My adventure was called –

I chose to –

I chose to –

My adventure

My adventure was called –

I was in a –

I saw a –

I felt –

My favourite
part was the –

My journey

My adventure was called –

On my way I saw –

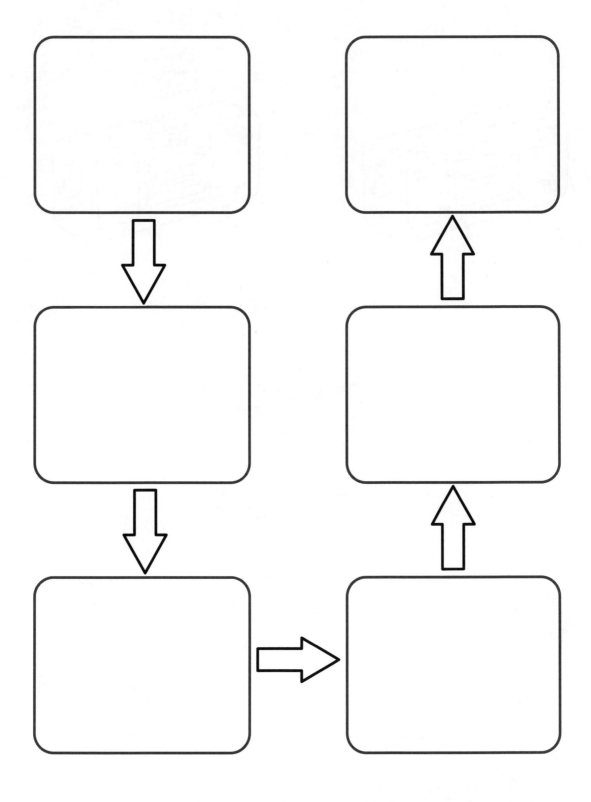

113

Cut out the pictures.
Put them in the right order to play the music.

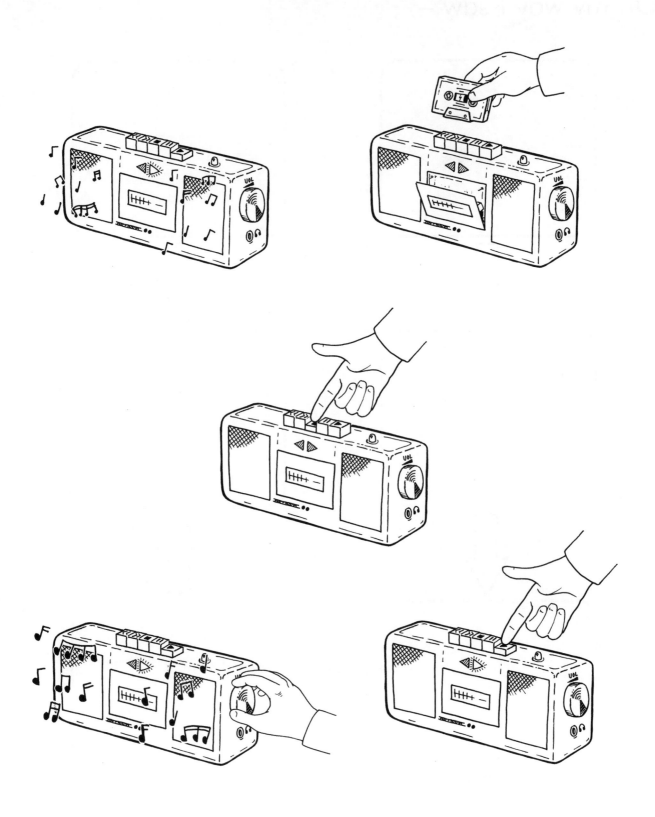

Working machines

These things can be controlled by computer chips.
Some of them could be worked by people.
Draw a person next to the ones that could be
worked by people.

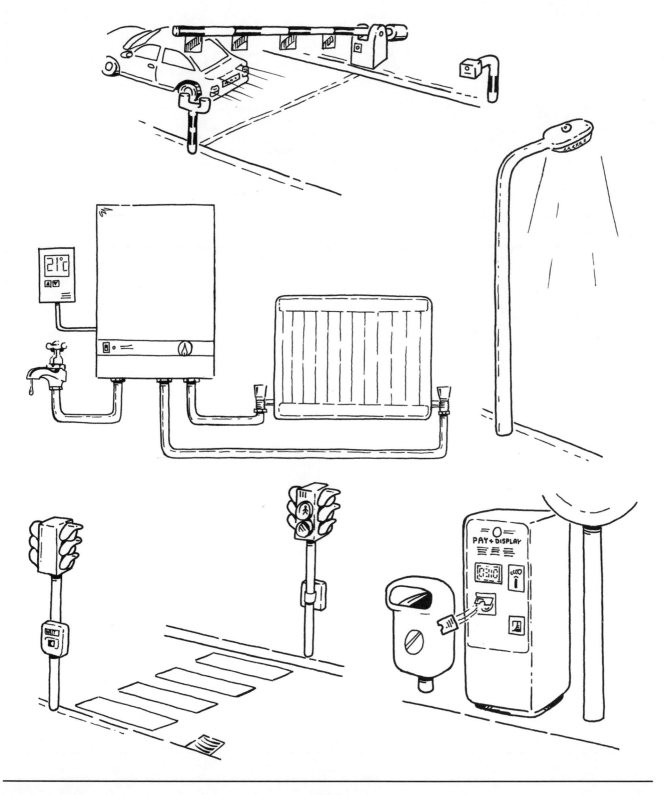

Use the computer to find something out.
Click on the words and pictures.
Draw some things you found.

I found a

I saw a

My favourite was

Look at the picture.
Colour the things which make a noise.

Use the CD-ROM to find information.
Use the A–Z index.

letter	word	sentence or picture
b		
h		
m		
r		
t		
w		

Using a CD-ROM

Explore the CD-ROM.
Record some things you found.

My favourite thing	A picture I found
Something I did not like	**A sound I found**

Use the maps on the CD-ROM.
Find the countries with the arrows.
Put the names of the countries in the boxes.

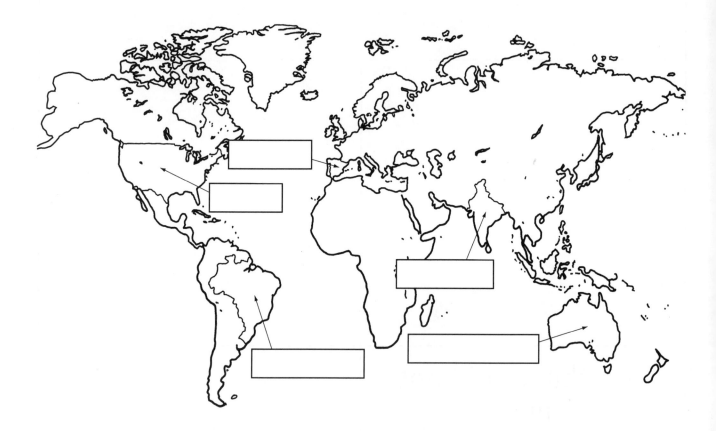

Use the CD-ROM.
Find Greenland. Label it.
Find Japan. Label it.

Use the CD-ROM.
Find video clips. Play them.
Make a list of them below.

Video clips I found	

World Wide Web

Draw a picture of something that you have seen on the World Wide Web.
Choose something that you have seen in real life.

I saw this on the World Wide Web. I have seen the real one!

I have explored a website.
I looked closely at the pages.

Name of website	
Colour of the pages	
Colour of the writing	
The button style	
I saw this picture	

Look at the two websites.

Search for information about what transport is used in each of these places.

Draw pictures of the forms of transport in the chart.

Place 1 is called _____	Place 2 is called _____

Design your own website.

Choose a topic to give you ideas for your site.

Fill in the title in your favourite colour.

Colour the background.

Make a special design for the buttons.

Write a title for each page (choose a colour for the writing).

Plan some pages for a computer presentation.
Choose a topic you like.
Fill in the titles for the three pages.
Draw some pictures for your pages.

Title – _____

Page 2 –

Page 3 –

1

Page 2 – _____

2

Page 3 – _____

3

Look at the other children's presentations.
Fill in the report sheet.

	Presentation 1	Presentation 2	Presentation 3
Title			
Background colour			
Text colour			
Pictures			

127